D0330709

PJ
TIME

100 DEVOTIONS TO LIGHT UP THE NIGHT

ILLUSTRATED BY
ELA SMIETANKA

Tommy
NELSON®

PJ Time

Published in Nashville, Tennessee, by Tommy Nelson. Tommy Nelson is an imprint of Thomas Nelson. Thomas Nelson is a registered trademark of HarperCollins Christian Publishing, Inc.

Illustrations by Ela Smietanka.

Tommy Nelson titles may be purchased in bulk for educational, business, fund-raising, or sales promotional use. For information, please e-mail SpecialMarkets@ThomasNelson.com.

Library of Congress Cataloging-in-Publication Data

Names: Smietanka, Ela, illustrator.
Title: PJ time : 100 devotions to light up the night / illustrated by Ela
   Smietanka.
Description: Nashville, Tennessee : Tommy Nelson/Thomas Nelson, [2020] |
   Audience: Ages 4-8. | Audience: Grades 2-3. | Summary: "Put on your PJs,
   grow closer to God, and drift off to sleep with PJ Time! Each devotion
   includes a fun nighttime theme, Bible verse, prayer, and reflection.
   Fascinating facts about the wonders of the night and bright
   illustrations of children in animal pajamas will make kids want to
   settle in at bedtime and rest in God's love"-- Provided by publisher.
Identifiers: LCCN 2019032044 | ISBN 9781400211272 (hardcover)
Subjects: LCSH: Bedtime prayers--Juvenile literature. | Christian
   children--Prayers and devotions--Juvenile literature.
Classification: LCC BV283.B43 P59 2020 | DDC 242/.62--dc23
LC record available at https://lccn.loc.gov/2019032044

Printed in China

20 21 22 23 24   LEO   10 9 8 7 6 5 4 3 2 1

Mfr: LEO / Heshan, China / January 2020 / PO #9557520

CONTENTS

1

MOON GLOW

"In the same way, you should be a light for other people. Live so that they will see the good things you do. Live so that they will praise your Father in heaven."

—MATTHEW 5:16

Have you ever seen a full moon? When the moon is big and round, it can light up the night.

But did you know that the moon doesn't have any light of its own? While the sun is a burning star, the moon is only a giant rock. Instead of shining its own light, the moon reflects the sun's brightness.

The Bible teaches that people are like the moon. By ourselves, we don't have any light. But when we stand in front of Jesus, the Light of the World, we can reflect His brilliance.

When we make Jesus our Lord, He puts His Spirit inside us. When Jesus is in us, we glow with His love and kindness, His truth and hope. From smiling at a new student to sharing a Bible verse to helping clean the house, we show the light of God when we share His love and truth.

Dear God, thank You for making the moon and the sun to give the world light. Help me shine Your light on others each day.

SHINE YOUR LIGHT INTO THE NIGHT!

Think of someone who needs a little love and friendship. How can you shine the light of Jesus into that person's life?

A BIG, SMELLY MESS

But the wicked are like those who stumble in the dark. They can't even see what has hurt them.

—PROVERBS 4:19

What's your favorite kind of sandwich?

Could you make your favorite sandwich in the dark? Could you find the bread? How well could you spread the mayonnaise or the peanut butter? You'd probably end up with a big mess! And you couldn't clean up in the dark either. Over time, your kitchen would smell like moldy bread and sour cheese.

Over and over, the Bible describes sin as darkness. When we do wrong, it's like we're living with the lights out, making a wreck of everything we touch.

People sin for all different reasons. Sometimes they are mad at God. Sometimes they are selfish. Sometimes people don't know God and what He says is right. Sometimes people just make mistakes. But the results are the same: a great big, smelly mess.

Jesus came to save us from the darkness of sin. When we ask for His forgiveness, He helps us clean up our messes. Then we can make beautiful things as we work in His light—and maybe even a sandwich or two.

Dear God, thank You for sending Jesus
to save us from the messes we make by
sinning. Help me see the ways I can live
in Your light and share it with others.

SHINE YOUR LIGHT INTO THE NIGHT!

Have you made a mess recently by doing something wrong? Ask Jesus to forgive you and to help you clean it up and make it right.

HOLD ON

But you are to hold fast to the LORD your God.

—JOSHUA 23:8 NIV

What position do you fall asleep in? Do you curl up on your side or lie on your tummy?

Otters sleep on their backs, floating in the water. They also hold hands as they drift off to dreamland. Clasping paws keeps otter families floating together.

Similarly, we can stay close to God by holding on to His truths. Hold on to the truth that God created you just right (Psalm 139:14). Cling to the fact that Jesus loved you enough to die on the cross as the payment for your sins (Ephesians 5:2). Squeeze your mind tight around the truth that God will never leave you by yourself (Deuteronomy 31:6).

As you learn more and more about the Lord, your grip will grow strong. It will become easy to hold on, just like those sleepy otters.

Dear Lord, I want to keep learning Your truths. Help me hold on to You and Your Word.

SHINE YOUR LIGHT INTO THE NIGHT!

Supplies: paper, crayons, Bible

What truth do you need to remember tonight? Ask an adult to help you find a Bible verse about something that is troubling you. (Or use a verse from this devotional.) Then write down the verse or draw a picture of it.

4

TOOTHPASTE TEST

As a tree gives us fruit, healing words give us life. But evil words crush the spirit.

—PROVERBS 15:4

What happens when you squeeze a tube of tooth-paste? Toothpaste comes out, of course! But what if you made a mistake and it's not time to brush your teeth? How do you put the toothpaste back in the tube?

Words are a little like toothpaste. As long as your words are inside your mind, no one can hear them. You can change the words or keep them to yourself. But once you let the words out, they won't go back in.

If we choose kind and encouraging words, we help other people. No one wants to give back encouragement! But when we say mean words that hurt people's feelings or tear them down, we harm others. And we'll wish we had never said those words in the first place.

When you feel mad, sad, or afraid, let your words out carefully. And when you're happy, thankful, and full of love, let those warm, sweet words sing!

Jesus, You always chose the best words to say to others. Please help me control my temper and only say words that please You.

SHINE YOUR LIGHT INTO THE NIGHT!

In what situations do you have the hardest time controlling what you say? The next time you're in that situation, stop and ask God to give you the right words.

I SEE YOU!

Ask the animals, and they will teach you. Or ask the birds of the air, and they will tell you. . . . Or let the fish of the sea tell you.

—JOB 12:7–8

Ouch! Have you ever crashed into something at night when you got up to get a drink of water? That's because God created people to see best during the day.

But lots of animals see best in the dark. Some, like the bush baby, have ginormous eyes. Big eyes let in more light and help these animals see in the dark.

Do you ever feel like God is in the dark and you can't see Him? Just like He gave the bush baby powerful eyes, He'll help you see Him in all kinds of places. You just have to look.

The Bible tells us that we can see God through the things He made. Have you ever seen something amazing in nature, like a snowfall, a soaring eagle, a gigantic shark, or a brilliant rainbow? Many things that make you say "wow!" allow you to see God with your spirit because He made them.

Ask God to help you see Him in nature every day. You'll be saying "wow!" a lot more often.

Jesus, I saw You today in the _____.
I can't wait to see You again tomorrow!

SHINE YOUR LIGHT INTO THE NIGHT!

Are you ready to see God at work in His creation? Choose an animal to learn about tomorrow.

CHILL OUT

Then they heard the Lord God walking in the garden. This was during the cool part of the day.

—GENESIS 3:8

B rrr! It can get chilly at bedtime as the sun disappears. In the Gobi Desert, the temperature plunges from 100 sweaty degrees in the daytime to 25 shivery degrees at night!

God created the daily cycle of sunlight and darkness, including the in-between evening time. In the garden of Eden, God enjoyed the evening by visiting His friends Adam and Eve.

Sadly, Adam and Eve disobeyed God one day. The next time God visited, they ran away. Their sin had messed up their friendship with God, and Adam and Eve were afraid.

God had to punish Adam and Eve, so He sent them out of the garden. But He continued to love them very much. And He made a plan so people could be friends with Him again. God sent Jesus to pay for our sins. Now everyone who loves and believes in Jesus becomes a friend of God. As the air cools tonight, chill out with the God who wants to be your friend.

Dear Lord, I'm so happy to be Your friend.
I know that I can tell You anything. I'm
excited that _____. I'm
sorry that _____.

SHINE YOUR LIGHT INTO THE NIGHT!

Come up with a plan to make time with God a daily habit. Is there a specific time in your day that you can give Him? Is there a habit you can start, such as singing a praise song when you get dressed or reading the Bible after snack time?

7

REARVIEW MIRROR

The Lord's love never ends. His mercies never stop. They are new every morning.

—LAMENTATIONS 3:22–23

You probably looked in the mirror as you brushed your teeth tonight. What did you see? If the mirror was big enough, you didn't just see your face—you saw whatever was behind you too. In fact, that's why cars have a rearview mirror. It helps the driver see what's behind the car.

Now think about your day like you are looking in the mirror to see what's behind you. How many great things happened today? Can you name at least five blessings? Did anything bad or sad happen?

Jesus cares about all of that—the good things and the bad things. So each night when you climb into bed, think back on everything that happened during the day. Thank God for the blessings. Tell Him about your problems and mistakes. And no matter what happened today, remember that tomorrow is a brand-new day full of adventures with Jesus!

Jesus, thank You for being with me today. Thank You for the blessings of _____ and _____. Help me with _____.

SHINE YOUR LIGHT INTO THE NIGHT!

What did you do today that God is proud of? What can you do tomorrow to make God proud?

8

STORYTELLER

Jesus again used stories to teach them.

—MATTHEW 22:1 NCV

What is your favorite bedtime story? Why?

Stories can be sweet, sad, exciting, or funny. Because stories are fun, they are easy to remember. We can picture the people and places in our minds.

Jesus was super smart, so He knew all about the power

of stories to help people understand. He used stories to tell people about God's ways.

One day, He told three stories. One was about a man who searched here and there and everywhere for a sheep that had wandered away. The next was about a woman who was happy after she found a lost coin. Then there was a father who celebrated when his runaway son came home. These stories show that God is full of joy when people who are "lost" without Him come to know and love Him.

Everyone loves stories, and everyone needs to hear about Jesus. Will you be one of Jesus' storytellers? You can start with the stories about the lost sheep, coin, and son from Luke 15.

Jesus, thank You for the stories You share with me through the Bible. Help me understand the truths the Bible teaches.

SHINE YOUR LIGHT INTO THE NIGHT!

Share one story about Jesus with the person who tucks you in tonight. Who can you share it with tomorrow?

9

WIN THE RACE

You know that in a race all the runners run. But only one gets the prize. So run like that. Run to win!

—1 CORINTHIANS 9:24

At night, cheetahs curl up in tree branches to snooze. Cheetahs are tuckered out at day's end because they hunt during the day, unlike other cats. When chasing prey, cheetahs sprint at speeds up to 70 miles per hour. That's as fast as a car on the highway! And just like any race, the cheetah gets a prize if it wins—dinner!

The Bible tells us that life is like a race. If we run the race the right way, we'll get a prize too. We'll get Jesus!

Do you run toward Him every day? You don't have to be super fast like the cheetah. Just keep going. Keep living for Jesus. Live for Him even when you're tired, upset, or mad. And every day, He'll be running right next to you, cheering you on. Jesus is a prize you can enjoy all the time!

When your race is finished, you'll win the best prize of all. You'll live with Jesus forever in heaven.

Dear Jesus, help me do better
at _____ so I will
keep traveling closer to You.

SHINE YOUR LIGHT INTO THE NIGHT!

Is anything making it hard for you
to follow Jesus? Ask an adult to help
you think of ways to keep your eyes
on Jesus and to run toward Him.

10

PILLOW THRONE

Feel free to come before God's throne. Here there is grace. And we can receive mercy and grace to help us when we need it.

—HEBREWS 4:16

Gather some extra pillows and stack them in a big pile on your bed. Find your favorite fuzzy blanket and lay it on top.

Then picture this: You are in a fancy palace. Your bed is a giant throne. Sitting on the throne is Jesus. Angels stand all around Him. Jesus opens His arms wide, and you crawl up into His lap. What do you want to tell Him?

In Psalms, we learn that King David often cried, praised, and told God everything from his bed (Psalm 63:6). There, he could meet alone with God.

God wants to hear from you too. Even though He is the King in charge of the whole world, He loves it when His children come to His throne room to talk to Him. He is never too busy! Climb up on your pillow throne, and tell Him anything and everything. Ask Him for whatever you need.

Jesus, You are the King. I'm so glad to be Your child! Thank You for listening to me. I want to tell You about _____.

SHINE YOUR LIGHT INTO THE NIGHT!

Think about tomorrow. Are you worried or excited about something? Do you need God's help with anything? Make a list or draw pictures of the things you think about.

11

ON TRACK

God is working in you to help you want to do what
pleases him. Then he gives you the power to do it.

—PHILIPPIANS 2:13

Whoo-whooooo! Have you ever heard a train whistle
in the night?

While you're sleeping, trains race across the land.
Trains have powerful engines that help them travel

hundreds of miles in one night. With all that speed, trains need solid, strong tracks. Even around curves and over hills, trains stay on course as their wheels cling to the tracks.

Do you know what is like both a train engine and the train tracks? God's Holy Spirit! If you follow Jesus, the Holy Spirit lives in your heart. The Spirit gives us God's power to be brave, to help others, and to feel God's special joy even in trouble. But the Spirit also keeps us on God's track by showing us what is right. The Spirit helps us go exactly where we're meant to go—closer toward Jesus.

Thank You for sending Your Spirit to give me power. Help me do right. Help me love You the best I can by _____.

SHINE YOUR LIGHT INTO THE NIGHT!

Supplies: paper, crayons

What helps you stay on God's track? Is it singing about Jesus, going to children's church, or hearing the Bible read out loud? Make a thank-you note for someone who shares one of these activities with you. Draw a train and write, "Thank you for helping me stay on track."

12

STINKY OR SWEET?

Our offering to God is this: We are the sweet smell
of Christ among those who are being saved.

—2 CORINTHIANS 2:15

What are some of your favorite bedtime smells? Soap?
Fresh sheets? Mom's perfume as she tucks you in?

The Bible says that we smell good to God when we love Him and love others. This means that we make Him happy and relaxed, just like the scent of fresh sheets or fruity-smelling soap makes us happy and relaxed.

The Bible also teaches that we're like a sweet smell to people who don't yet follow Jesus. People can sense that there's something different and special about us, even though they don't know quite what it is. But we know. We belong to Jesus! We're learning to act like Him, look like Him, and think like Him

Don't be stinky! Love God and show His love to others. Be a sweet smell to everyone around you.

Jesus, I want others to "smell" You
when they're around me. Teach
me how to be more like You.

SHINE YOUR LIGHT INTO THE NIGHT!

What can you do to be a
"sweet smell" tomorrow?

13

A HAND IN THE DARK

When I am afraid, I will trust you.

—PSALM 56:3

Close your eyes. Now wave your hand in front of your face. Did you see your hand move?

Caves are so dark that you can't see what's right in front of you, even with your eyes wide open. When people explore caves, they bring lights to see the way.

Sometimes life can feel like a deep, dark cave. You can't see what's next. You don't know what direction you're traveling.

But what if your parent was in the cave with you? They would hold your hand and lead the way. You still wouldn't be able to see, but wouldn't you feel better? Holding on to a parent makes our fear go away because we have a good leader.

God is the best leader, *and* He can see in the dark! When we have to try something new and scary—like moving to a new house, visiting the doctor, or making new friends—it might feel like we're walking in the dark. But God is with us, and He knows the way! If you hold on to Him, you will make it back into the sunshine.

God, thank You for leading me. I know I'm safe with You. You can see the path even when I can't.

SHINE YOUR LIGHT INTO THE NIGHT!

How can you help someone with a fear? Maybe you can hold your sister's hand when you pass the neighbor's barking dog. Or perhaps you can close the door tightly so bugs don't get in the house and frighten your brother.

14

ELEPHANT HUGS

Then Jesus took the children in his arms. He
put his hands on them and blessed them.

—MARK 10:16

Did you know that elephants use their trunks to hold
hands and hug? Elephant parents love to cuddle their
little ones. Touching is one way that elephants show they
care about each other.

Touch was important to Jesus too. One day, a group

of children wanted to see Jesus. His friends told them to go away, but Jesus said, "What are you doing? Bring them here!" Then He took the children into His big, strong arms. He placed His hands on them, and He prayed for them. Jesus also showed His love when He healed sick people by touching them.

We can't touch Jesus until we get to heaven, but He gives us people on earth to love and cuddle. Who can you share God's love with by wrapping them up in an elephant-sized hug?

Dear Jesus, I am excited to hug You when I get to heaven! Thank You for giving me people to cuddle with here on earth.

SHINE YOUR LIGHT INTO THE NIGHT!

Supplies: lotion

Touch Mom or Dad's hand. How does it feel? Then relax while they rub lotion on your hands. Doesn't that feel wonderful?

15

FUZZY, SQUISHY THOUGHTS

Brothers, continue to think about the things that are good and worthy of praise. Think about the things that are true and honorable and right and pure and beautiful and respected.

—PHILIPPIANS 4:8

Quick! Think about your favorite bedtime things. There are fuzzy stuffed animals, soft pajamas, cozy blankets, and smooth sheets. Maybe you love your fat, squishy pillow or your night-light that glows like a star. Now don't you feel cozy and ready for bed?

Our thoughts are powerful. They can change how we feel and what we do. The Bible says the more we think about God's truths, the more our minds think like His mind. When we listen to music that praises God, we think about how great He is. When we read the Bible, we start to view people like their loving Father views them. Before long, we love God and His people more. God's truth changes our minds for the better. And then our actions become more like His actions.

Fill your mind with thoughts as fuzzy as your stuffed animal, as squishy as your pillow, and as bright as your night-light. Your heart and actions will quickly follow.

Dear heavenly Father, I think You're awesome. Train my mind to think just like You!

SHINE YOUR LIGHT INTO THE NIGHT!

Supplies: paper, pencil

Write down three reasons it's good to help around the house. Tomorrow, read the list before doing your chores. Getting the work done will be much easier!

16

STAND LIKE A FLAMINGO

You will be able to stand strong. And when you have finished the whole fight, you will still be standing. So stand strong.

—EPHESIANS 6:13–14

Can you sleep standing on one leg all night long? You'd probably topple over! But flamingos snooze with one leg tucked against their bellies.

In the Bible, the apostle Paul said to stand strong. But he wasn't talking about sleeping like a flamingo. Paul was talking about standing for Jesus—being strong in what you believe about Him. If you know that Jesus is kind and loving and no one can change your mind, you are standing strong.

Standing for Jesus also means behaving in a way that matches what you believe. Standing for Jesus is serving God even when you're tired. It's doing the right thing even when you really want to misbehave.

Any time you feel weak, ask Jesus to give you strength. He'll help you stand strong like a silly pink flamingo!

Dear Lord, give me Your strength.
I want to stand strong for You.

SHINE YOUR LIGHT INTO THE NIGHT!

Do your friends ever ask you to do something wrong? How can you stand strong for Jesus and do the right thing the next time that happens?

17

TREASURE HUNT

"The kingdom of heaven is like a treasure hidden in a field. One day a man found the treasure, and then he hid it in the field again. The man was very happy to find the treasure. He went and sold everything that he owned to buy that field."

—MATTHEW 13:44

Do you have a belonging that is extra special? Maybe it's your favorite blanket, a stuffed animal, or a book from Dad.

There's nothing wrong with having favorite toys. But God wants you to have real treasure too—the kind of treasure that changes your life and makes you jump up and down with delight. You won't need to dig up this treasure from a field or pull it up from a sunken pirate ship though. In fact, it's super easy to find. It's Jesus!

Jesus is more valuable than anything else you can imagine. You can be unhappy if you have money or power or fame—or all three. But your heart will spill over with joy when Jesus lives there, no matter what else you have.

What's even better than a treasure chest full of all the toys in the world? A heart full of Jesus' joy and love and a sure future with Him in heaven. So go on a treasure hunt and dig up Jesus. Then share your riches with everyone you meet.

Dear Jesus, You are extra special. Help me love You more than the things I want, such as _____ and _____.

SHINE YOUR LIGHT INTO THE NIGHT!

The Bible tells us a lot about how extra special Jesus is. Read Acts 4:12. Why is Jesus the greatest treasure?

A SAFE PLACE

The LORD is my rock, my fortress, and my savior; my God
is my rock, in whom I find protection. He is my shield,
the power that saves me, and my place of safety.

—PSALM 18:2 NLT

Have you ever climbed all the way under your covers to
sleep? Then you've made your bed a little like a fox den.
A den is a cozy underground tunnel where foxes live. Fox

dens keep out the cold. They also keep little foxes safe from danger. To sleep, fox siblings curl up in a big, furry heap inside the den.

Just as foxes have dens, people have a safe, cozy place. But it isn't dark or underground. And you'll never find it in the woods, no matter how hard you look.

God Himself is our place of safety. He is always with us, and He is a mighty guard! Sometimes we go through hard times. We get sick, or we feel scared. But we don't have to handle these things by ourselves. God promises to surround us with His loving arms of safety and peace.

When you get scared or sad, go to God and curl up in His safety.

God, I feel safe knowing that You
are my protector. I don't need to be
afraid of _____.
I know You are always with me.

SHINE YOUR LIGHT INTO THE NIGHT!

Do you ever worry when you go to school? When you meet new people? When the lights turn off at night? Remember, God is surrounding you with His perfect love.

BATH MATH

With God's power working in us, God can do much, much more than anything we can ask or think of.

—EPHESIANS 3:20

What's the difference between an ordinary bath and a bubble bath?

Bubbles, of course! The bath math is simple: add the right kind of soap to the bath water, and you're surrounded with suds!

The same kind of amazing math happened in the Bible—but not with bubbles. One day while Jesus was teaching, the crowd got hungry. A boy wanted to help, so he gave his lunch of five rolls and two fish to Jesus. Jesus multiplied that meal to be enough food for more than five thousand people! That's God's kind of math. He can take the smallest thing and use it to bless many, many people.

Have you ever wanted to help someone but felt as if you didn't have anything big enough to matter? No gift is too small for God to use. Be like the boy in the story, and give what you have. When you have a giving heart, He will use you in bigger ways than you could ever imagine!

God, thank You for bubbles and all Your blessings. Help me see when I can bless someone else. And use Your amazing math to make that blessing big.

SHINE YOUR LIGHT INTO THE NIGHT!

Supplies: crayons, colored paper

Think of someone you want to bless, and make that person a card. Write a note or draw a picture of the boy who gave his lunch. Your little card will make a big smile!

20

LITTLE BRANCH

"I am the vine, and you are the branches. If a person remains in me and I remain in him, then he produces much fruit. But without me he can do nothing."

—JOHN 15:5

How would you like to sleep with your head smooshed into your own stinky armpit?

That what a sloth does! At bedtime, a sloth hangs

by his long claws. His feet snuggle together, and his furry head tucks under an armpit. Nothing bothers him because he's almost invisible. He looks just like a branch!

You're like a branch too. And Jesus is your big, strong vine. Think about it: The branches of a vine get everything they need to grow and live from the vine. Without the vine, the branches can't do anything. But when they're attached to the vine, they grow big and produce leaves and fruit.

Do you see how you're like the branch? You get everything you need to grow and live from Jesus. Without Him, you can't do anything. But when you're stuck to Him, you can be kind and loving to people. You can have joy in your heart and live in a way that's pleasing to Him.

All you must do is stay connected to the true Vine!

Jesus, I need You for everything in my whole life! Help me stay close to You.

SHINE YOUR LIGHT INTO THE NIGHT!

Supplies: paper, pencil

Brainstorm a list to finish each sentence.

The vine is _____.

The branch is _____.

21

LIGHTEN YOUR LOAD

"Come to me, all of you who are tired and
have heavy loads. I will give you rest."

—MATTHEW 11:28

Have you ever gone on a vacation or spent the night
at Grandma's house? If so, you probably packed a

suitcase or backpack for the trip. Toothbrush? Check. Clothes? Check. Favorite stuffed animal? Check. But what if you also packed a pile of books, a jug of juice, and a baseball bat? Your bag would be way too heavy to carry!

Jesus tells us that many people carry weights that are too heavy for them. And that heavy load makes them so tired! Jesus wasn't talking about suitcases though. He was talking about how heavy we feel when we worry about something we can't fix.

Do you have worries that are too heavy for you? Lighten your load! Get rid of that extra weight by telling an adult and then telling Jesus. And trust Him to take care of it! He is strong enough to carry all your problems.

Dear Jesus, sometimes I worry about
_____. Please carry that problem
for me. I trust You to take care of it.

SHINE YOUR LIGHT INTO THE NIGHT!

Are there people you know who have been sad lately? Help them carry their heavy sadness by being a good listener. Then tell them about Jesus, the best listener.

PENGUIN HUDDLE

"If two or three people come together in
my name, I am there with them."

—MATTHEW 18:20

Quick, what's a roost? Don't know? Well then, what's a rookery?

Roost and *rookery* are funny words that both describe a group of birds sleeping huddled together. A group of penguins is a rookery. A group of crows is a roost.

Crows like to be alone during the day, but they gather together at night. These types of birds are smart! They know they need each other to stay warm.

People need each other too. We need each other in order to learn. How would you know how to share if there was no one to share with? How would you learn to wait patiently if you were always first? Most of all, we need our friends and family to help us learn about Jesus.

Guess what? Other people need you! They need your smile and the special things you do. You help others learn about Jesus just by being you.

So thank God for all the wonderful penguins—oops, *people*—in your life!

Dear Jesus, sometimes I get upset
with others. Help me remember that
I need them and they need me.

SHINE YOUR LIGHT INTO THE NIGHT!

To appreciate people is to be thankful for them. Choose one person you'll see tomorrow, and tell him or her, "I appreciate you!"

23

INCH BY INCH

The little child began to grow up. He became stronger and wiser, and God's blessings were with him.

—LUKE 2:40

Did you try to grow today? Probably not! But when you ate fruit, drank water, and got ready for bed, you were working on growing.

If you stare at yourself in the mirror, you won't be able to tell that you're growing. But it's still happening—even while you sleep! You are growing so slowly that you don't notice it until later.

God says that our spiritual hearts grow the same way. Just like good food, water, and rest help our bodies grow, we grow stronger spiritually when we feed our souls. As you pray, praise, read the Bible, and make kind choices, God is growing you up. You will grow step by step and inch by inch—just like Jesus grew when He was a child. So keep learning about Him. And keep practicing what He says to grow a strong and wise heart.

God, thank You for helping my body and soul grow big and strong. Teach me how I can help others grow stronger in You too.

SHINE YOUR LIGHT INTO THE NIGHT!

How can you help someone else grow?
Maybe you can give your pets fresh water,
be a good example to your siblings,
or share a Bible story with a friend.

24

NIGHT-LIGHT

[Jesus] said, "I am the light of the world. The
person who follows me will never live in darkness.
He will have the light that gives life."

—JOHN 8:12

Did you know that some fish glow in the dark?
The anglerfish lives in the deepest oceans where
there's no light. On the head of female anglers is a long

spine that looks like a fishing pole. At its end, a shimmering little ball lights up the water like a night-light bulb.

When Jesus lives in your heart, He's like your very own night-light. Just as a night-light helps you find the bathroom without bumping into things, Jesus shows you the right way and helps you see danger.

By praying and reading the Bible, Jesus' light inside you will grow brighter. When you feel like doing the wrong thing, He'll light up the darkness. If you're thinking about being mean to a sibling, He'll remind you what His Word says. And He'll show you how to be helpful, not hurtful. Just like the anglerfish's night-light, Jesus' love glows bright!

Jesus, You're the Light that shines inside me. Fill me with even more of Your light so I can _____.

SHINE YOUR LIGHT INTO THE NIGHT!

Supplies: night-light

Turn off every light in your room, and close the shades. Then turn on a night-light. What a difference it makes! What a difference *Jesus* makes when He lives in your heart!

25

WASHED CLEAN

But if we confess our sins, he will forgive our sins. We
can trust God. He does what is right. He will make
us clean from all the wrongs we have done.

—1 JOHN 1:9

Have you ever been covered in mud? Perhaps you played
in a puddle. By the time you came inside, the mud had
dried and coated your skin like glue. Yuck!

When you're really dirty, there's nothing to do but climb into the bathtub. After a few minutes soaking in the warm water, that sticky, glued-on mud washes right off.

Jesus tells us that water can help us understand what happens to our hearts when we bring our mistakes to Him. We may feel like our sins are stuck to us like dried mud on our knees. Maybe we're scared to admit we need help. But when we tell Jesus the truth and ask for His forgiveness, He makes us clean. If you sin, don't let it get hard on your heart. Take it to Jesus right away. He will gladly wash you clean.

Dear Jesus, I feel dirty because I
_____. Please forgive me.
Thank You for making me clean again!

SHINE YOUR LIGHT INTO THE NIGHT!

Think about your day. Did you say or do anything that made your heart a little muddy?

26

TOPSY-TURVY

"These men who have turned the world
upside down have come here."

—ACTS 17:6 AMP

Did you know that manatees sleep upside down? That's
right! These wonderful creatures sleep in the water,

but they breathe air. So they flop over onto their backs to sleep. They rest their flippers on their round bellies and point their noses up above the water's surface.

Sometimes being topsy-turvy is a good thing. Jesus taught people to live in an upside-down way. It's easiest to think only about ourselves, but Jesus said to put others first. He taught us to love those who dislike us instead of trying to get even. He said to always tell the truth instead of lying and to be humble instead of bragging.

When Jesus' followers began teaching others what He had taught them, some people didn't want to live differently. "These men are turning the world upside down!" they fussed. But Jesus' friends happily and bravely kept obeying God by teaching the truth.

Do you put yourself first, or are you a topsy-turvy manatee living as Jesus taught?

Dear Jesus, it's hard to be different. Give me courage to do things upside down like You did.

SHINE YOUR LIGHT INTO THE NIGHT!

What can you do this week to live in a topsy-turvy way like the first Christians did?

27

WISE WISH

If any of you needs wisdom, you should ask
God for it. God is generous. He enjoys giving to
all people, so God will give you wisdom.

—JAMES 1:5

If you could have anything in the world when you wake
up tomorrow, what would it be?

In the Bible, God asked King Solomon that question.
Solomon could have asked God to make him rich. He

could have asked for a big army. Or he could have asked to live a long life. But out of all the tempting choices, Solomon asked God to make him wise.

Solomon wanted to be a good king. He wanted to do a good job leading God's people. God was so pleased with Solomon's choice that He made him wiser than anyone else in the world.

So what does wisdom look like? It isn't knowing facts or doing well in school. True wisdom means understanding God's ways and living by them. As you read God's Word, the Holy Spirit will help you understand God's ways. He will also give you strength to obey God's words. Wisdom is one of God's favorite gifts, so ask Him to give you His wisdom today!

Lord, I want to make good choices. Please make me wise like Solomon so I can _____. Thank You!

SHINE YOUR LIGHT INTO THE NIGHT!

Look up Proverbs 29:11. What is one thing that a wise person does? Are you wise?

28

BEAUTIFULLY DIFFERENT

The sun has one kind of beauty. The moon has
another beauty, and the stars have another.
And each star is different in its beauty.

—1 CORINTHIANS 15:41

There are 250 billion stars in the Milky Way galaxy. That
number looks like this: 250,000,000,000. Wow!

God created each star, and He made them all different *and* beautiful. Two stars can both be wonderful even though they're nothing alike. It's the same with animals and people.

But sometimes we want everyone to be just like we are. It's easier if our friends like the same things we do. If you want to draw but your friend wants to play tag, you have to *try* to get along. But this doesn't mean either of you is wrong.

The next time you feel mad at someone, stop and ask yourself if the person is being mean or just being different. Then remind yourself that God thinks you're both awesome. You are both beautifully different!

Jesus, help me be patient and kind when other people are different from me.

SHINE YOUR LIGHT INTO THE NIGHT!

Supplies: construction paper, crayons, scissors

Draw a star on a piece of paper and cut it out. Then decorate the star in your own special way. Your star will be different from any other star in the whole world, just like you are.

29

WHOOOO WILL GO?

I heard the Lord asking, "Whom should I send as a messenger to this people? Who will go for us?" I said, "Here I am. Send me."

—ISAIAH 6:8 NLT

Way up in the treetops at night, owls hoot to one another. Turning their big, feathery heads this way and that, they call out as if to ask, "Whoooo's there?"

One day, God asked the same thing. He called out,

"Who? Who will go and give a message to My people?" A man named Isaiah quickly said, "I'll go!" Today, God still asks that question of all His children: "Who will go and give My message?"

There are lots of people in the world who serve and love God. There are also many who don't know about Him but who need Him just as much! This is why God needs messengers who will tell others about Him. Some messengers travel long distances to faraway countries. We call these people missionaries. But just as often, God sends His messengers to the house next door.

You see people every day who need to know more about Jesus. Will you be His messenger?

Dear Lord, I'll be Your messenger. Send me!

SHINE YOUR LIGHT INTO THE NIGHT!

Supplies: paper, pencil, crayons

Ask Mom or Dad to help you write a note of encouragement to a missionary or a person who spreads God's message. Draw a pretty picture on the letter.

30

A LULLABY FOR YOUR HEART

God, my strength, I will sing praises to you. God, my protection, you are the God who loves me.

—PSALM 59:17

Have you ever fallen asleep while someone sang to you? After a busy day, a peaceful lullaby can help you fall asleep in minutes.

King David understood the power of music to calm, bring joy, and help him through trouble. David wrote lots of songs, many of which you can read in the book of Psalms. When David was sad, he sang to God to feel better. When he was happy, he sang to share his joy with God. When he was scared, he sang songs about how much he trusted God. Singing helped David feel rested and strong again.

Singing songs to God is another way to talk to Him. God created music, so it makes sense that singing can bring peace and quiet to our hearts. When we sing about His goodness and love, we remember that nothing on earth can separate us from Him.

Jesus, thank You for Your goodness and peace. Thank You for always listening to my songs.

SHINE YOUR LIGHT INTO THE NIGHT!

Make up your own song about your dearest friend, Jesus. Sing it to Him, and you'll soon be full of joy and peace.

31

I'M LISTENING!

Listen to the word of the Lord. Open your
ears to hear the words of his mouth.

—JEREMIAH 9:20

All seems quiet at night. TVs and computers go silent. People stop talking and laughing. Even your pets settle down.

But not everything hushes at night. Sit still and listen.

What do you hear? Chances are you heard some sounds you weren't expecting—maybe some you've never noticed before. You heard them because you were listening.

In the Bible, a young boy named Samuel heard a sound one night. At first, he thought it was his caretaker, Eli. But it wasn't. Three different times Samuel heard a voice calling his name. Finally, he realized it was God's voice. Samuel answered God, "Speak, Lord. I am your servant, and I am listening" (1 Samuel 3:10). Then God told Samuel an important message.

Do you ever wonder what God has to say to you? Ask Him to speak. And be sure to listen by reading the Bible, asking wise friends for advice, and praying.

Lord, I want to hear You, and I am listening. Help me hear Your voice.

SHINE YOUR LIGHT INTO THE NIGHT!

Supplies: Bible, paper, pencil

Read John 3:16 out loud. Then say or write the verse using your own words. Do you understand God's message a little more?

32

LOVE LIKE A RAIN CLOUD

They are like clouds blowing over the
land without giving any rain.

—JUDE V. 12 NLT

Pitter-patter, *splish, splish, splash!* Do you like the sound
of rain at night? It's like a lullaby from God.

God created clouds to give rain to the earth, to

people, and to animals. Without rain, our lakes would dry out, and we wouldn't have water to drink. We wouldn't be able to grow vegetables or grain to eat. We couldn't even wash our stinky feet. If clouds blow around in the sky but don't give rain, they are useless.

People can do the same thing. When we have something to give but keep it to ourselves, we are being selfish. God gives people all kinds of different gifts, and He wants us to share them. He might give you time, money, artistic talent, or a big heart. Whatever your gifts are, rain them down on others like a spring shower that makes everything bright and green. God made clouds to give rain, and He made people to shower down His love.

Jesus, You're the most generous of all! Help me be like You: never selfish and always giving.

SHINE YOUR LIGHT INTO THE NIGHT!

Think of something you have that you can give away—maybe a toy car that's still like new or a cool shirt you outgrew too quickly. Ask Mom or Dad if you can drop it off at a collection box tomorrow.

33

YOU'RE WELCOME

Jesus said, "Let the children come to me. Don't stop them! For the Kingdom of Heaven belongs to those who are like these children." And he placed his hands on their heads and blessed them.

—MATTHEW 19:14–15 NLT

What would happen if you knocked on your best friend's door right now? Would your friend's parents welcome you inside to play?

Even with our friends, there are good times to visit and bad times to visit. But there is never a bad time to visit Jesus!

One day when Jesus was teaching, some parents tried to bring their children to Him. Jesus' disciples thought it was a bad time. Jesus was busy. He was teaching adults about God's kingdom. And He was healing sick people. The disciples told the parents to take the kids away. But this made Jesus angry. He welcomed each child and blessed them all.

You are so important to Jesus! Even though you are young, Jesus loves to spend time with you. It doesn't matter where you're from or what you've done—Jesus wants to be your friend. You are always welcome to visit Him!

Jesus, thank You for always being with me. Help me be a good friend to others by making them feel welcome.

SHINE YOUR LIGHT INTO THE NIGHT!

Think about the other children you played with today. Is there anyone you ignored or left out? How can you make that person feel welcome tomorrow?

34

YUM!

Taste and see that the Lord is good.

—PSALM 34:8 NIV

What's your favorite bedtime snack? Some kids just love sweet treats, like juicy peaches or yogurt. Others would rather have something salty, like popcorn or nuts. And then there are other flavors, like earthy mushrooms, tangy herbs, and sour candy.

God has given us a whole world of tasty foods to try. And He made our tongues in a special way so that we can taste them. Each taste bud on your tongue has tiny hairs that send signals to your brain about what you're tasting.

God wants us to enjoy the amazing world He has made. And He wants us to enjoy Him as the giver of great gifts. When we taste the sweetness of a strawberry or the richness of spaghetti sauce, we are getting a small taste of God's goodness! We can also taste His goodness through other gifts, like a friend's kindness or a parent's love. As you enjoy God's great gifts, remember to thank Him for being so sweet.

Father, thank You for Your goodness. You are so sweet to me!

SHINE YOUR LIGHT INTO THE NIGHT!

Think of two things you could tell someone to show God's sweetness. Then think of two things you could do to show that person God's sweetness. Make sure to act on one of your ideas tomorrow.

35

WONDERFULLY MADE

I praise you because you made me in an amazing and
wonderful way. What you have done is wonderful.

—PSALM 139:14

Do you ever take naps that last for weeks . . . and weeks . . .
and weeks? Of course not! But snapping turtles do.
Snapping turtles can sleep for *months* at a time. When
the weather turns cold, they wiggle down into the mud at

the bottom of a pond and go to sleep. That's because God made snapping turtles in an awesome and special way. Their bodies and shells can soak up enough oxygen from the water to breathe until springtime.

Everything God has made is wonderful, including you. He's never made a person and then said, "Oops!" He always does it right the first time.

Think about the things your body can do. Do you have legs that can kick a ball? Can your brain add numbers and learn to spell new words? Do you have hands that can draw dinosaurs and superheroes?

God made you in an amazing and wonderful way!

Dear God, thank You for making me in an amazing way. I'm so happy that I'm able to _____.

SHINE YOUR LIGHT INTO THE NIGHT!

Think about all the body parts you have just from the neck up: eyes, ears, nose, tongue, brain, teeth. Choose one, and then list some of the great things you can do with that part.

36

BRUSH UP

God, examine me and know my heart. Test me and
know my thoughts. See if there is any bad thing
in me. Lead me in the way you set long ago.

—PSALM 139:23–24

What did you see in your mouth when you brushed your
teeth tonight? Teeth, foamy toothpaste, your pink
tongue? How about six billion bacteria? No?

You didn't see the bacteria because they're too tiny. But they are still there! That's why brushing is important. It keeps our teeth and gums healthy and strong.

Nasty thoughts are a lot like those teeny bacteria. You can't see them, but they can hurt you if you don't clean them up. In the Bible, King David asked God to help him find any bad thoughts. David wanted his thoughts to be sparkly clean and pleasing to God. But he wasn't sure he could see the dirty thoughts by himself, so he asked God for help.

Sometimes our bad thoughts are invisible to us. We get angry or proud, and we can't see the truth. Ask God to help you find those icky thoughts. And when He shows you one, be sure to ask Him for forgiveness. He'll scrub it away.

God, You can see things in my heart that I can't see. Help me remember anything I've done, thought, or said today that needs cleaning. Thank You for Your forgiveness.

SHINE YOUR LIGHT INTO THE NIGHT!

One way your thoughts can become yucky is by being jealous of a friend who has a new toy. Can you think of two more ways?

37

A GIFT TO GROWN-UPS

Children are a gift from the Lord. Babies are a reward.

—PSALM 127:3

How do skunks get any sleep? Can't they smell each other?

Believe it or not, skunks don't smell bad all the time. If something is bothering them, they can spray on purpose and everything will stink. But usually, they smell just fine.

Well . . . *most* of the time. Once in a while, a young skunk will accidentally spray (especially if something surprises him). Then the whole den smells skunky!

Sometimes it's tough being young. You want to do things as well as the adults and the big kids do, but that's not always possible. Sometimes accidents happen. But that's okay. God knows (and so do parents!) that there's much to learn when you're a child.

Children are very special to God. He says you are a gift from Him to the grown-ups in your life. When God watches you, He smiles. He thinks you're amazing.

Dear God, sometimes it's hard for me to do things as well as I want to, like _____.
Thank You for helping me learn!

SHINE YOUR LIGHT INTO THE NIGHT!

Jesus loves every single child on earth. The next time a friend, sibling, or classmate makes a mistake, love that person like Jesus does and be patient.

38

SING, SHOUT, OR SIGN

All of you who fear God, come and listen. I will tell you what he has done for me. I cried out to him with my mouth. I praised him with my tongue.

—PSALM 66:16–17

Have you ever spent a night camping in the woods or by a lake? Then you know that nature can be noisy! Birds sing, crickets chirp, and coyotes yip. Each animal speaks the language that God gave it. God knows what every creature is saying, and He loves listening to each one.

God also loves to listen to us. Whether we pray silently or out loud, in English or Arabic, He understands every word. Even when you sob or cheer, God hears the words of your heart. Some people even talk to God using hand signals. This is called sign language.

Whether we sing like the birds or sign with our hands, God hears us. When we talk silently in our hearts and when we chat with God out loud, He understands. No matter how you talk to Him, God wants to hear from you because you are His child.

Jesus, I'm so glad You like listening to me and that You always understand me. I love You.

SHINE YOUR LIGHT INTO THE NIGHT!

Make a fist. Now point your thumb, your pointer finger, and your pinky out, keeping your two middle fingers down against your palm. This hand signal means "I love you" in American Sign Language. Make the sign for Jesus. Tomorrow, teach your family how to say "I love you" without saying a word.

39

HEAD TO TOE

"God even knows how many hairs are on
your head. So don't be afraid."

—MATTHEW 10:30–31

Anybody can count sheep to try to fall asleep. Tonight,
try a bigger challenge. Count all the hairs on your
head. What? Are there too many?

It would probably take all night to count every hair—if

you could keep track that long. That's because most people have around 100,000 hairs on their heads.

But you don't need to count your hairs. God already knows. He also knows where that scab is and how that other kid treated you today. God knows everything about you because He made you and He watches over you.

So no matter what happens in your life, don't be afraid. God already knows all about it. And don't worry that your problems are too small or too big for Him to handle. From the top of your head to the bottom of your toes, God cares about everything that matters to you because you matter so much to Him!

God, I'm amazed that You know everything about me and You still love me. Thank you for caring for me.

SHINE YOUR LIGHT INTO THE NIGHT!

Supplies: paper, crayons

Draw a picture of yourself. Draw at least twenty curly or straight lines for your hair. Think about how big God must be to know just how many hairs are on your real head—and everything else about you.

40

DONKEY IN DANGER

Remember, it is sin to know what you
ought to do and then not do it.

—JAMES 4:17 NLT

Don't sneak up on a donkey at night!

Donkeys' eyes are set far apart, so they can see all around them. Donkeys can see their four legs and anything behind them—all at the same time! So if anything sneaks up behind them, donkeys know. They kick their powerful legs and run away.

Like a coyote creeping up to a donkey, sin can sneak up on you. You know you should mind your parents, but you choose to do what you want. Or your friend makes fun of the new kid, and you crack a joke too. Or you tell a little lie to stay out of trouble—which turns into a bigger lie and then a bigger one.

Suddenly you're feeling yucky in your heart. You know Jesus sees exactly what you're up to! It's time to say, "No more!" Tell an adult the truth, and ask Jesus for forgiveness. You'll be back on track in no time.

Be a donkey when it comes to sin. Kick and run when it tries to sneak up on you!

Dear Jesus, I know I should _____,
but sometimes I choose to _____.
I'm sorry for sinning. Thank You so
much for Your forgiveness!

SHINE YOUR LIGHT INTO THE NIGHT!

Is there a sin that's been sneaking up
on you lately? Talk to Jesus about it.

41

COME IN!

Remember to welcome strangers into your homes. Some people have done this and have welcomed angels without knowing it.

—HEBREWS 13:2

Have you ever given up your bed so a guest could sleep there? It might feel uncomfortable to share your space, but God loves it when we make others feel welcome. That's called *hospitality*.

Sometimes showing hospitality means having guests for dinner. Other times, it can be sitting with someone and talking. The main idea is to make others feel loved and cared for.

Showing hospitality is important because people can feel God's love for them through our kindness. The Bible even says that sometimes guests are actually angels in disguise! How cool is that?

No matter who comes to visit, try to make them feel at home. If having guests makes you shy or nervous, that's okay. Ask a parent to help you practice what to say before your guests arrive. Then just do your best. God will smile at you as you show hospitality and share His love.

Lord, I want people to feel welcome when they are with me. Help me think of ways I can share Your love with others.

SHINE YOUR LIGHT INTO THE NIGHT!

Hospitality is a big word, but it's simple to carry out. You might get your guests a glass of water or ask them if they'd like to sit down. Can you think of one more way to show hospitality?

42

THE CASE OF THE MISSING THANK-YOU

Give thanks whatever happens. That is what
God wants for you in Christ Jesus.

—1 THESSALONIANS 5:18

Imagine a beautiful Christmas tree with shiny presents
all around. Children in pajamas race into the room and
tear open the wrapping paper. They squeal with delight

as they open their gifts. Then they take their new toys to their rooms to play the rest of the day.

As wonderful as this story sounds, something is missing.

All the children received great gifts, but none of them remembered to thank the gift giver. The same problem happened once to Jesus. One day, He healed ten men who were sick with a terrible skin disease. But only one man said thank you. Only that man pleased Jesus.

Whether someone gives you a present at Christmas, shares their chips with you at lunch, or compliments your science project, don't forget to say thank you to the person and to God. God loves thankful hearts!

Jesus, You are the best gift giver ever. Thank You so much for _____.

SHINE YOUR LIGHT INTO THE NIGHT!

Name one person who gave you a gift today. What kind of gift can you give him or her a gift tomorrow?

43

MAKE ME A LIGHTNING BUG, PART 1

When you talk, do not say harmful things. But say what people need—words that will help others become stronger.

—EPHESIANS 4:29

Have you ever chased lightning bugs after dark? These wonderful little creatures are also called fireflies. They're bright like fire and lightning, but they're harmless. They don't bite, and they don't have pincers.

There are many ways to harm people with our words. We might hurt their feelings through something we say or by yelling instead of speaking kindly. We might even tell a lie. But Jesus wants our words to be as harmless as lightning bugs and also just as pleasing. Just as lightning bugs add joy and beauty to the nighttime, we can add kindness everywhere we go.

Practice being harmless when you're playing with others. If your friend shows you her painting and you don't like it, don't say, "That's ugly." Instead, say, "Thank you for showing me your picture." Don't speak unkindly and harm others. Use words that help. Be a lightning bug!

Jesus, help me say things
that make people smile.

SHINE YOUR LIGHT INTO THE NIGHT!

Supplies: flashlight

Make the flashlight blink like a lightning bug. Does it make you happy when the light blinks? Think of two ways you can make someone smile with a flash of kindness tomorrow.

44

MAKE ME A LIGHTNING BUG, PART 2

The Jewish leaders saw that Peter and John were not afraid to speak. . . . They were amazed. Then they realized that Peter and John had been with Jesus.

—ACTS 4:13

Scientists can tell a lot about a lightning bug just from the way its little light blinks on and off. Different types of lightning bugs blink at different speeds and using different patterns. Scientists can tell one type of lightning bug from all the others by its blinking light.

Are you like a lightning bug? People should see that we're Christians because we're caring and joyful. In tonight's Bible verse, the leaders knew that Peter and John were followers of Jesus because of the way they spoke. They were different from most people. They had lots of wisdom. They weren't afraid or embarrassed to talk about Jesus. The leaders could tell right away that these men had spent time with Jesus.

If someone watched you all day long, would that person know that you're a Jesus-following bug?

Jesus, I want people to be able to tell that I follow You. Help me use words and actions that shine like You.

SHINE YOUR LIGHT INTO THE NIGHT!

Think back on your day. In what ways did you look like someone who spends time with Jesus?

45

THE WHISPERING WIND

There are things about God that people cannot see—his eternal power and all the things that make him God. But since the beginning of the world those things have been easy to understand. They are made clear by what God has made.

—ROMANS 1:20

One moment, all is quiet and calm in your room. Then suddenly you hear a *whooooosh* rushing outside. Trees groan and scratch. Leaves rattle like maracas. You don't see anything out your window, but you know what it is. *It's just the wind*, you think.

We can't see wind, but we know it's there. It moves the trees, leaves, and flags. It blows our hair and jacket.

Seeing and believing in God is like seeing and believing in the wind. We can't see Him with our eyes, but we can see the world He has made. We see amazing animals and kind people. We see sky-high mountains and endless oceans. We can't see His form because God is a Spirit, but we watch His wonderful work happening all throughout the universe.

Tonight, know that God is as real as the wind. And remember that the same God who made the whole giant universe is with you right now in your room. Let His love warm your heart as you drift off by His side.

Father, I can't see You, but Your world shows me how amazing You are. Thank You for making _____ and _____.

SHINE YOUR LIGHT INTO THE NIGHT!

Where is your favorite place to play outside? Make a list of all the things in that place that show God is real.

46

CLEAN NESTS

The earth and everything in it belong to the Lord.
The world and all its people belong to him.

—PSALM 24:1

Before a mother bird goes to sleep at night, she cleans her nest. She clears pebbles, uneaten food, and other trash. She even carries her chicks' droppings away in a little sac! This keeps the baby birds clean so their wings can get fluffy and strong for flying.

God is pleased when birds take care of their nests. That's one of the jobs He has given them. And just like birds' nests, God gives us little pieces of His world to care for.

The Bible tells us that God put people in charge of all He made. People, plants, and animals are all part of His wonderful creation. He wants us to enjoy them, but it's also our job to take care of them. When we feed our pets, water the plants, clean our rooms, or pick up trash, we make the world a better place. So hop to it, birdie! Clear out those pebbles, and make God's world a little more beautiful.

Jesus, thank You for all the blessings
You give me to enjoy. Help me do
my part to take care of them.

SHINE YOUR LIGHT INTO THE NIGHT!

What can you take care of tomorrow
to keep God's world beautiful?

47

NEVER A WASTE

Always give yourselves fully to the work of the Lord.
You know that your work in the Lord is never wasted.

—1 CORINTHIANS 15:58

We sure spend a lot of time sleeping! Again and again, we end our day the same way: crawling into bed to sleep the whole night through. Does that seem like a big waste of time?

Believe it or not, sleep is not a waste of time. When you're sick, sleep helps your body become healthy and strong again. Damaged muscles heal, and cuts and bruises fade away. Your brain takes a break from solving problems. Even your memory gets better.

Even though it seems like we're doing nothing when we sleep, our bodies are doing all kinds of helpful things. In the same way, it can seem like we aren't doing much when we take time to pray, read the Bible, or listen to a friend who's sad. But these quiet activities are actually important work for God. They help us, and they help the people around us.

Taking time for Him and for others is always important work. Nothing you do with a joyful heart is ever wasted!

Dear Jesus, I'm so happy that every minute
I spend with You is time well spent.

SHINE YOUR LIGHT INTO THE NIGHT!

What did you do for the Lord today?
What can you do tomorrow?

PAID FOR

The payment for sin is death. But God gives us the
free gift of life forever in Christ Jesus our Lord.

—ROMANS 6:23

Have you ever broken something that didn't belong
to you?

Sometimes we make mistakes that we can't fix.
Maybe you broke a friend's tablet, and you don't have
the money to buy a new one. Maybe you forgot to let the

dog out, and she chewed up the table leg. It feels terrible when we do something wrong and we have no way to make it right.

Each time we sin, we break our friendship with God. And we can't make that right by ourselves. But that's why Jesus died on the cross. His death pays what we owe for our sins.

Other people may get mad when you do something wrong. But God will forgive you in an instant for anything, tiny or huge. All you have to do is ask because Jesus already paid for it.

We can't fix our wrongs, but God gives us a new start through faith in Jesus.

Jesus, thank You for dying on the cross to pay what I owe for my sins. I am so glad You are alive again and want to be my friend. I need Your help with _____.

SHINE YOUR LIGHT INTO THE NIGHT!

Is there anything that you need Jesus' help to make right?

49

JUST FOR FUN

Our Lord and God! . . . You made all things. Everything existed and was made because you wanted it.

—REVELATION 4:11

It's always dark deep in the ocean.

If you were to travel straight down into the sea, you would end up in pitch blackness. No light from the sun shines that deep into the water. This part of the ocean is called the "midnight zone." Yet there are fish, squid, and other creatures living down there in the dark!

Few humans ever travel that deep. That means there are many sea animals that no one will ever see except God. So why did He make them? Why didn't He just leave the midnight zone empty?

God made these creatures for Himself. He created many things for us to look at and enjoy, but some are just for Him—just for fun. All the marvelous fish, birds, plants, mountains, and oceans are here because He wanted them.

What a big, big God you serve! No star is too far away. No mosquito is too small. No fish is too deep. There's nothing that He can't see.

Dear God, I know You enjoy all the things You've made. Help me take care of this world and remember that You love it.

SHINE YOUR LIGHT INTO THE NIGHT!

What does it say about God that He made creatures just so He can enjoy them?

50

JUICY SWEET

But the Spirit produces the fruit of love,
joy, peace, patience, kindness, goodness,
faithfulness, gentleness, self-control.

—GALATIANS 5:22–23 NCV

Have you ever taken a bite into a rotten apple? You were expecting it to be crisp and sweet, but instead it was way too soft, and the taste was . . . ew!

It's easy to know when food is good or bad. It's not as easy to know whether a person is good or bad though. You can't take a bite of them to find out! But you can watch what they do. Jesus said that you can tell which people belong to Him by how they act.

When people love God, they just can't help being sweet because His Spirit lives in their hearts. The Bible calls this sweetness "the fruit of the Spirit." People can tell that we're sweet God-followers when we have love, joy, peace, patience, kindness, goodness, faithfulness, gentleness, and self-control.

Don't be a rotten apple. Ask God to help you grow the fruits of the Spirit. Then everyone around you can see the juicy sweetness of Him.

Holy Spirit, thank You for growing God's fruit in my heart. Show me which fruit I need to work on the most. Use my life to help other people see how sweet You are.

SHINE YOUR LIGHT INTO THE NIGHT!

Choose one of the fruits of the Spirit in today's verse. Did you show that fruit to others today? How can you show it tomorrow?

51

BY NAME

Look up to the skies. Who created all these
stars? . . . He calls all the stars by name.

—ISAIAH 40:26

Hurry! Look out your window, and count all the stars in
the sky!

Did you count them all? Of course not! There are too
many for anyone to count. Even the person who's better
at math than anyone else in the world would never be

able to do it. But God knows each one. What's more, He has named them all!

He knows your name too. In the Bible, God tells us that He has called us by name because we belong to Him.

God made you—from your eyeballs to your tummy to your toes. Since He's your Maker, He knows more than just your name. He knows everything about you! He even knows what you're thinking right this minute. You can trust that the One who knows your name also loves you and will take good care of you.

God knows your name—but even better, He knows *you*. And He wants you to know *Him*!

> Dear Lord, it makes me feel safe
> and special that You know my name
> and everything else about me!

SHINE YOUR LIGHT INTO THE NIGHT!

How does it make you feel to know
that God calls you by name? Think of
two people who need to know that
God knows their name. Next time you
see them, share the good news.

52

PIECE-MAKER

A gentle answer will calm a person's anger. But
an unkind answer will cause more anger.

—PROVERBS 15:1

Imagine that there is only one piece of pie left. You really want it, but your brother or sister asks for it too. How can you make your sibling happy without missing out on dessert?

Be a piece-maker! Oh wait, that should be *peace-maker.* If you cut the pie in two, you will both have a piece of dessert to enjoy. And your family will have peace.

A peacemaker helps others calm down by finding a way to solve problems. A peacemaker helps two people who are separated by anger or disagreement make up and be friends again.

Jesus is the best peacemaker of all because He solved the problem between God and people caused by sin. Sin makes it hard for us to be friends with God. It's like a disagreement with Him about what is right. But Jesus solved the sin problem by paying for our wrongs on the cross. If you follow Jesus, He takes away the sin that separates you from God.

God, I don't want to cause fights. I want to be a peacemaker like Jesus. Teach me to calm myself down when I'm angry.

SHINE YOUR LIGHT INTO THE NIGHT!

Do you often get angry or upset around someone—maybe a brother, sister, or classmate? Think of the first gentle step you can take to bring calm and peace.

53

WHEN THE SUN STOPPED

The Lord says: I have an agreement with day and
night. I agreed that they will continue forever. Day
and night will always come at the right times.

—JEREMIAH 33:20

Day and night will always come at the right times," says
God. But one day, it didn't happen!

Long ago, Joshua and the Israelite army were in a

battle. They faced five evil kings and their armies all at the same time. Joshua needed more time, so he prayed, "Sun, stand still. . . . Moon, stand still." And it happened! "The sun stopped in the middle of the sky" until Joshua's army defeated the bad guys (Joshua 10:12–13).

Why did God bend His own rules? Because someone prayed. That's how much it means to Him when we pray.

When you pray, God listens. He thinks about what you've said and decides how to answer. Sometimes He says no because He has something better for you. Other times He says yes because He loves to give His children gifts. Most important of all, He wants to hear from you. What will you ask Him today?

Dear God, please help my family with _____. Thank You for hearing every prayer. We trust You to do what's best for our family.

SHINE YOUR LIGHT INTO THE NIGHT!

Ask your parents if there's something they've been asking God to do. Add your prayers to theirs, and see what happens.

54

GOD'S SERVANTS

But during the night, an angel of the Lord opened
the doors of the jail. He led the apostles outside.

—ACTS 5:19

Are angels real?

One night, God sent an angel to help some of

Jesus' followers escape jail. Verses like this one show us that angels are very real!

Long ago, God created many angels and gave them jobs. Day and night, angels travel all over the world, doing God's work. Some angels are messengers. Some angels are worshipers in heaven. Some angels are warriors. Some angels take care of people. When Jesus was on earth, angels cared for Him when He was hungry and tired.

Angels aren't chubby little babies like you see in some pictures. Rather, they are powerful and strong. But they are also gentle and full of love. Angels always obey God and serve Him. Sometimes that means opening locked jail doors, and other times it means watching over you.

Dear God, thank You for creating angels.
I can't wait to meet them one day!

SHINE YOUR LIGHT INTO THE NIGHT!

How do you feel knowing that
God sends powerful, loving, and
wise angels to take care of us?

PATIENCE PRACTICE

A wise person is patient.

—PROVERBS 19:11

What are you looking forward to? Perhaps it's a class trip, a birthday, or a family member's visit. But what if God made a miracle, and you got what you wanted this very moment? All of a sudden, you're boarding the bus for the class trip or getting out of bed on your birthday. If that happened, you'd be super excited, right? But . . . you'd also be very tired after skipping tonight's sleep!

We'd rather get what we want right now. But God says waiting is a good thing. He knows what we really need, and He knows the best time to give it to us. When we are patient, we show God that we trust Him.

God also wants us to be patient with other people. He wants us to give others the time they need without getting angry. That's how He treats us, after all. So whether you are waiting on God or people, ask Him to fill you with patience.

Jesus, it's so hard to wait to get what I want. Please help me notice when I'm impatient, and teach me how to wait.

SHINE YOUR LIGHT INTO THE NIGHT!

Life is full of waiting—at the store, at the playground, and at the doctor's office. Think of two ways to pass the time while waiting for your turn.

56

TOO MUCH!

Try to avoid going too far in doing anything. Those who honor God will avoid doing too much of anything.

—ECCLESIASTES 7:18

Desert snails can sleep for a *looooong* time!

If the weather gets too dry or cold, desert snails will burrow underground. They curl up in their shells with their eyeballs tucked inside their heads. Then they sleep for up to four years!

Sleeping is cozy, but four years would be way too much sleep for a person.

Many things are nice unless we want too much of them. For example, watching TV can be a good way to relax. But too much TV time will cause you to forget how much you like playing outdoors. Video games are lots of fun—unless you play so often that you don't spend time with your parents or brothers and sisters. One donut is wonderful, but three will give you a bellyache.

Thank God for all the wonderful gifts He's given you by using them the right way. That means stopping when you've had enough. And always remember that He is the greatest gift of all!

Dear Jesus, sometimes I want too much
_____. Help me honor You by
stopping when I need to stop. Thank You!

SHINE YOUR LIGHT INTO THE NIGHT!

Think of two more things that are
fun unless you have too much. What
do you often want too much of?

57

KINDNESS FOR ALL

May the Lord show you his kindness.

May he have mercy on you.

—NUMBERS 6:25

Did you meet anyone new this week? Maybe there was a new kid at soccer practice, or one of your dad's friends came to your home.

Meeting people we don't know can be a little scary. We're not sure what to say, or we're afraid the person won't like us. But if the new person is kind, something amazing happens—we instantly feel better.

In the Bible, Jesus was kind to all people. It didn't matter if they were rich or poor, healthy or sick, popular or left out. Jesus cared about everyone. He showed His love by talking to people and helping them.

Jesus' acts of kindness still help people today. When we read about them in the Bible, we remember His love. And we can follow His example. So keep an eye out for opportunities to be kind, and spread that comforting feeling everywhere.

Jesus, thank You for being kind to me. Please help me care about others the way You do.

SHINE YOUR LIGHT INTO THE NIGHT!

Did someone do something kind for you today? What kind thing can you do tomorrow for a friend or family member?

58

SIESTA TIME

[Jesus] said to them, "Come with me. We will go to a quiet place to be alone. There we will get some rest."

—MARK 6:31

Can you believe that in some countries grown-ups take a nap every day?

In places such as Spain and Mexico, everyone stops what they're doing in the middle of the day to nap. These naps are called *siestas* in Spanish. Even the busiest men and women take siestas. Why? Because even grown-ups need to stop and rest sometimes.

Your parents love taking care of you. They keep your clothes clean and folded. They buy food at the grocery store and then cook your favorite meals. But sometimes moms and dads get tired. Taking care of a family is hard work!

Aren't you grateful for all the things your parents do for you? One way to thank them is to make their work a little easier. For example, you could offer to fold the washcloths. Or you could carry the grocery bags in from the car.

Let your parents know you think they're amazing. And the next time one of them sneaks a siesta, fetch them a pillow!

Jesus, thank You for all the things my parents do to take care of me. Help me learn how to help them more, and bless them with good rest.

SHINE YOUR LIGHT INTO THE NIGHT!

Are you ready to help your parents rest? Ask Mom or Dad how you can help with one meal tomorrow.

COUNT ON HIM

Lord, you are a God who shows mercy and
is kind. You don't become angry quickly.
You have great love and faithfulness.

—PSALM 86:15

When it's time for bed, who tucks you in? When you go
to school, who teaches you? When you are sick, who
can you count on to help you?

God puts special people in our lives who take care of us every day. When someone keeps on doing what's right day after day, he or she is *faithful*.

Even an animal can be faithful. Several years ago in China, there lived a little dog named Wang Cai. He always sat outside the bank where his owner worked. Each day, Wang Cai waited for his owner. Then the little dog kept his master company all the way home.

The Bible tells us that God is more faithful than anyone else. Thousands of years ago, He was powerful, loving, and perfect. He's still that way today. He won't ever leave you or be mean to you. Each day, you can count on Him to keep you company and love you. Just don't expect Him to wag His tail!

God, I can always count on You to do what's right. Please help me obey You each day so I can become faithful too.

SHINE YOUR LIGHT INTO THE NIGHT!

Are you faithful like Wang Cai? Do you stay close to Jesus day after day? When it's hard to trust or obey, remember that He is always faithful to you!

60

FEEDING JESUS

"I was hungry, and you gave me food. I was
thirsty, and you gave me something to drink."

—MATTHEW 25:35

What do bears, chipmunks, bats, box turtles, garter
snakes, hedgehogs, and wood frogs have in common?
Every winter, they snuggle up in a warm spot and go to
sleep—or hibernate—for a long, long, long, long time!

When an animal hibernates, its heart slows way down. It breathes oh so slowly, and it sleeps very deeply. Animals hibernate so that they can snore right through the months when food is hard to find.

Like bears and chipmunks in winter, some families have a hard time finding food. Some kids don't look forward to breakfast when they go to bed at night because they know there won't be any. This makes Jesus sad, and He wants us to help.

Jesus told His friends to show His love to others by sharing food. Then He said that when we share our food with those who don't have enough, it's exactly the same as sharing with Jesus Himself.

God didn't make people to hibernate. He made family, friends, and neighbors to help when food is hard to find.

Jesus, I want to show Your love by taking care of people in need. Help my family see when we can help someone.

SHINE YOUR LIGHT INTO THE NIGHT!

Ask Mom and Dad if they know someone who needs help. Plan to take a bag of food to that family.

61

TRIPLE DELIGHT

You are God's children. That is why God sent
the Spirit of his Son into your hearts. The
Spirit cries out, "Father, dear Father."

—GALATIANS 4:6

Do you sleep with a cup of water by your bed? Water is amazing! In your cup, water is in liquid form. But if you heat water up really hot, it turns to steam. Steam is water that has turned into a gas. And if you put it in the freezer or outside on a cold day, it changes into solid ice.

Just like water has three forms—liquid, gas, and solid—God also has three forms. The Father, the Son, and the Holy Spirit are the three persons of God. All three persons have different roles, but They are still just one true God!

Before our world was ever created, the Father, Son, and Holy Spirit lived together and loved each other. When God created people, He invited us to become friends with all three persons. Then Jesus, the Son, came to earth to rescue us from our sins. The Holy Spirit lives inside the heart of every child of God. The three persons of God still live together and love each other in heaven. But now, They also live with us. And all three persons love you very much!

Father, thank You for loving me. Jesus, thank You for dying for me. Holy Spirit, thank You for living in my heart.

SHINE YOUR LIGHT INTO THE NIGHT!

Can you name the three persons you just read about? Which one would you like to understand better? Ask Him to teach you about Himself this week.

62

STAR MAP

The Lord says, "I will make you wise. I will show you where to go. I will guide you and watch over you."

—PSALM 32:8

Long ago, sailors used the stars to find their way across the oceans at night. One star—the North Star—always stays in the same place while the others circle around it in the sky. Sailors knew where each star should be depending on the season. God had given them a giant map!

God has given you a map too. The Bible shows us who God is, what is right and wrong, and how to get to heaven. The Bible always points to the truth.

Any time you need to know the way, search the Bible for the right direction. If you want to find out if it's ever okay to lie, you'll discover that God hates lies (Proverbs 12:22). If you wonder whether God will forgive you for that awful thing you did, read Romans 8:38–39 and know that nothing can separate you from God's love.

God has given you a map that will always point you in the right direction. Learn to use it. Then full speed ahead, sailor!

Dear Jesus, thank You for the Bible.
Help me follow its map toward You.

SHINE YOUR LIGHT INTO THE NIGHT!

What do you want to know about God
or His plan for you? Ask an adult to
help you find the answer in the Bible.

63

ALL DAY, ALL NIGHT

He who guards you never sleeps.

—PSALM 121:3

Do you think you could sleep with one eye open? Probably not! But ducks can.

When it's time to go to sleep, a group of ducks lines up in a row. The ducks in the middle of the line close their eyes. But the two ducks on the ends of the row each keep one eye open. This way, they can watch for danger and protect each other.

Just like snoozing ducks, we have someone looking out for us. God is our protector! He is big and powerful. In a gazillion years, He has never worried about anything. Nothing in the whole universe frightens Him even a tiny bit. That's why we, His children, have nothing to fear either.

God doesn't have to sleep with one eye open to protect us at night. In fact, the Bible tells us that He doesn't sleep at all. We're safe all day and all night long because He watches over us.

Dear God, it's wonderful to know
that You are always wide awake
and protecting me. Thank You!

SHINE YOUR LIGHT INTO THE NIGHT!

Think of a few ways you can be a good protector tomorrow. Can you watch your little brother at the playground or take care of a pet? Be like God and protect others.

64

IT'S ALIVE!

God's word is alive and working. It is sharper than a sword sharpened on both sides. It cuts all the way into us, where the soul and the spirit are joined. It cuts to the center of our joints and our bones. And God's word judges the thoughts and feelings in our hearts.

—HEBREWS 4:12

Do you have anything alive in your room? Maybe you have a pet fish or a dog or cat who likes to sleep with you. Perhaps you have a plant in your window. Living things are different because they breathe and grow (even plants!).

Did you know that the Bible is alive too? God's Word isn't like any of the other books on your shelf. The words printed inside came from God. He told each human writer exactly what to put on the page. And the words are full of spiritual food and truth to help you grow. When we read God's Word and follow it, God's Spirit helps us understand who God is, what He is saying, and what He wants us to do.

Do you want to be full of life too? Then spend time each day reading the Bible, and ask God to make you more like Him.

Jesus, thank You for the Bible. Each
time I read it, help me learn more about
You and what You want me to do.

SHINE YOUR LIGHT INTO THE NIGHT!

Read one of these verses: Psalm 118:24, Luke 6:31, or Philippians 4:4. Do they remind you of anything in your life or something you learned at church? Tell an adult about it.

65

CAMPOUT

Our homeland is in heaven, and we are waiting for our Savior, the Lord Jesus Christ, to come from heaven.

—PHILIPPIANS 3:20

Have you ever gone camping? Camping includes some fun activities, like stargazing, building a fire, and roasting hot dogs and marshmallows. And it's exciting to spend the night outside with just a tent separating you from the world.

Camping is fun, but you wouldn't want to live in a tent forever. You'd start missing your house's heat and air conditioning. You'd wish for the solid walls that keep out the wind and rain. You'd want running water and lights.

The Bible says that living on earth is a little like camping in a tent. And heaven is our solid, warm, and safe forever home. Heaven is so much bigger and better than any house on earth. And if you follow Jesus, you will be there forever, which is a very long time!

That's why it's not important to have fancy houses, new toys, or nice clothes. We can't take those things to heaven. But we can take our friendship with God. And we can also take other people home with us if we tell them about Jesus.

Lord, I'm glad You made a home for me in heaven. Help me bring others home to heaven with me.

SHINE YOUR LIGHT INTO THE NIGHT!

Who do you need to tell about Jesus so they can have a home in heaven one day?

66

"FATHER, FORGIVE THEM"

Be kind and loving to each other. Forgive each
other just as God forgave you in Christ.

—EPHESIANS 4:32

Your little sister did it again! She keeps using your towel.
When you get out of the bath, it's already wet. Family
members are wonderful and frustrating! They can be our

friends for life. They can also get on our nerves and make us angry.

God wants us to forgive others and live in peace with them. He doesn't say it will be easy. But with His help, we can do it. Whenever you have a hard time loving or forgiving someone, remember what Jesus said on the cross: "Father, forgive them" (Luke 23:34). Jesus was being killed by people who hated Him, but He still forgave them.

Jesus can help you forgive too. The first thing to do when you're mad at someone is to ask Jesus to change your heart. He can help you love others like He does. Then pray for that person. Ask Jesus to help both of you follow Him better. And remember that you need forgiveness sometimes too.

Father, thank You for forgiving me when I mess up. Please help me share Your love and forgiveness with _____.

SHINE YOUR LIGHT INTO THE NIGHT!

Think of the last time you got mad at someone. Do you still feel even a tiny bit angry? Ask God to help you forgive that person.

67

GOD'S SPECIAL PLACE

You should know that you yourselves are
God's temple. God's Spirit lives in you.

—1 CORINTHIANS 3:16

I'm not going to bed until I get the job done!" said King David.

David badly wanted to build a place for God to meet with His people. David didn't actually stay awake until the temple was built though. He said this because he understood how important it is for people to spend time with God. David was a good king.

Long ago, people usually worshiped God in special buildings. But since then, Jesus came to earth, died for our sins, and went back to heaven. Today He lives inside each person who follows Him! Our hearts are now God's special place.

This means it doesn't have to be Sunday for us to worship Jesus. And we don't have to be inside a special building. We can spend time with God at any time and in any place. You can worship Him in the backyard, in your favorite chair, or in bed. You can even worship God while watching cartoons or taking a bath! *You* are the place Jesus lives now.

Dear Jesus, I'm so happy You live in my heart instead of in a building. I want to be a good home for You.

SHINE YOUR LIGHT INTO THE NIGHT!

What kind of home do you think Jesus wants? What can you do to make your heart that kind of home?

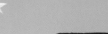

SNOWY WHITE

Take away my sin, and I will be clean. Wash
me, and I will be whiter than snow.

—PSALM 51:7

Does it snow in the winter where you live? You may go
to bed one night, your yard looking normal with bare
trees and brown grass. But in the morning, gleaming
snow covers everything like a beautiful white blanket.
The morning sunlight bounces off the snow and makes

the whole world seem brighter. It's as if your old house and neighborhood are gone. Now you have a beautiful white wonderland outside your window.

In the Bible, God talks about the beauty of snow. He says it's like the miracle that happens in our hearts when we confess our sin to God. No heart is too dirty for Him. He takes our sin and washes it away completely. When God is done cleaning us, our hearts are even whiter than beautiful snow.

So as you climb into bed tonight, don't worry if you messed up today. Just tell God about it. Then ask Him to change your heart. Every morning with God is beautiful because we get a fresh, new, snowy-white start.

Jesus, tonight I want to confess
_____. Please forgive me.

SHINE YOUR LIGHT INTO THE NIGHT!

Supplies: white chalk, black paper

Draw a snowy scene with the chalk and paper. As the white chalk covers the black paper, think about God's forgiveness making your heart bright and clean.

69

THE ZOOMIES

Sing a new song to him. Play well and joyfully.

—PSALM 33:3

What has four feet, a bushy tail, and goes zoom while everyone else is asleep? A cat!

Cats love to sleep all day and then play all night. Many cat owners have been awakened by their kitties rocketing up and down the hallway. There is even a name for this silly behavior: the cat zoomies.

Have you ever been so happy that you got the zoomies? That big, wonderful feeling is called *joy*. It's a gift that God gives His children because He loves them.

You probably feel joy when you're playing with Dad, your best friend, or Grandma. But you can also feel it when you're resting. That's because God's joy comes from knowing you are loved. The Bible teaches that if you want even more joy, just say, "Thank you." Thank Jesus for the things He's given you and the people He has put in your life. Thankfulness and joy go together—just like cats and the zoomies.

Jesus, thank You for all the blessings You give me, especially _____ and _____.

SHINE YOUR LIGHT INTO THE NIGHT!

Practice joy right now. Lie back, close your eyes, and make a list in your head of all your favorite things and people.

70

MIRROR IMAGE

Then God said, "Let us make human
beings in our image and likeness."

—GENESIS 1:26

Do you like to draw pictures? It's fun to see how crayons and markers can turn white paper into art. Even if you're not a great artist, your creations show a little bit about how special you are.

Did you know that God is an artist too? He loves to

create and design amazing things. Want to see one? Go look in the mirror.

Before you were ever born, God thought about you. He decided the shape of your nose and how many freckles to give you. He picked your hair and eye color. He even designed your personality! God says that all people are made in His image. It's like we are little mirrors reflecting how beautiful, and creative, and different God is!

Take time tonight to think about the way God made your mom, dad, family, and friends. Are you the same or different? Celebrate the special way He made each person. Then ask God how you can let others know how beautiful they are to Him too.

God, thank You for making me special
and different. I want others to see
You when they look at me.

SHINE YOUR LIGHT INTO THE NIGHT!

Fill in the blanks in this sentence: I am thankful for my _____ because I can _____. One example is "I'm thankful for my legs because I can climb trees."

71

YOU'RE RICH!

My God will use his wonderful riches in Christ
Jesus to give you everything you need.

—PHILIPPIANS 4:19

How much money do you have? Empty your piggy bank and count it up.

So are you rich or poor? Even if you have enough

money for a new toy or some candy, you probably don't have enough to buy a house, a car, or even a week of groceries.

Aren't you thankful your parents supply everything you need to live, learn, and grow? Most of the time, you don't even need to ask for what you need. They just do what they love doing best: they care for you.

God feels exactly the same way. He loves being our heavenly Father and taking care of us. God can meet all our needs. He gives us food, clothes, and shelter through our families. And He meets our spiritual needs for love and truth. As God's children, we are rich in His blessings!

What do you need today? Put away your piggy bank, and ask God. He will be glad to share His rich love with you.

Father, I have everything I need
because I belong to You. Tonight I want
to ask for help with _____.

SHINE YOUR LIGHT INTO THE NIGHT!

Can you think of five things you needed today that God gave you through your parents and others? Whose needs can you help God take care of tomorrow?

72

IMAGINE THAT

So we set our eyes not on what we see
but on what we cannot see.

—2 CORINTHIANS 4:18

Where can you tell jokes to a giant purple chicken while zooming through the sky on a flying T. rex over an ocean of chocolate? Only in your dreams!

Dreams come from your imagination. When you're asleep, your imagination takes over, and you can be anywhere! When you're awake, your imagination can be just as powerful. You can pretend to be a race car driver, make up interesting stories, or create sandcastles.

Creating things is awesome, but your imagination can do even more. You can even use your imagination to be like Jesus! When you see someone being teased, imagine how he is feeling. This will help you be kind and comforting. If you know an elderly person who lives alone, imagine chatting with her about your day and how happy this would make her. Then go do it!

What will your imagination dream up tonight? The sooner you fall asleep, the sooner you'll find out!

Dear God, sometimes I like to pretend that I'm _____. Thank You for giving me an imagination!

SHINE YOUR LIGHT INTO THE NIGHT!

Supplies: paper, crayons

Imagine you're playing tag with Jesus. Draw a picture of what you see.

73

A TOOTHY HUG

"Those who are sad now are happy.
God will comfort them."

—MATTHEW 5:4

How would you like to curl up and sleep in an alligator's mouth? That's what baby alligators do!

Gators look mean and scary, but they make great

moms. To keep her little ones from danger, a mother alligator scoops them into her mouth. The babies feel safe in their mom's big, toothy "hug."

Just like little alligators, we need comfort when we get upset or scared. A big hug tells us that we're safe. Kind words calm our hearts. All people feel better when they know they are loved and not alone.

Sad times will come, but we're never alone. Jesus is always with us. And He puts people in our lives to show us His love. Best of all, He promises that one day, in heaven, all sadness and pain will disappear. We will feel only joy with Jesus then!

Jesus, I can't wait to see You in heaven and feel Your hug around me! Help me see when other people need comfort. Help me show them Your love.

SHINE YOUR LIGHT INTO THE NIGHT!

Would you like to feel Jesus' love right now? Do you want to share His love with someone? Do both by giving a family member a great big hug!

74

HUNGRY HEARTS

"Those who want to do right more than anything else are happy. God will fully satisfy them."

—MATTHEW 5:6

Rumble rumble! What's that sound? It's not thunder. It's not a truck or a plane. It's the sound of a hungry tummy letting you know it's time to eat!

When we are really hungry, we get this strange feeling inside. We know that feeling means we need to eat something. Then we feel better.

God says the same is true for our hearts. We are happy when we feed on God's Word. We are strong when we follow what God says. Our hearts are actually hungry for right living, just like our tummies growl for food!

When we pray or read the Bible, we get energy to live the right way. The more we feed on God, the better we feel and the more we want to live like Him. So listen closely to your heart. Is it growling for what's right?

Jesus, make me hungry for right. Help me see all the ways I can live right for You.

SHINE YOUR LIGHT INTO THE NIGHT!

Supplies: paper, crayons

On one side of a piece of paper, draw your favorite food. On the other side, draw yourself doing something kind. Are you as hungry to do the right thing as you are for the treat?

155

75

THE PERFECT SHEPHERD

The Lord is my shepherd. I have everything I need. He gives me rest in green pastures.

—PSALM 23:1–2

Through the darkness, a lamb bleats. She is alone and afraid. Then someone scoops her up. He carries her back to the flock. She is safe because the shepherd is watching over her.

Many animals are fine on their own. But sheep don't

do well wandering around by themselves, even in groups. Sheep aren't very good at protecting themselves from wolves or coyotes. They often wander away and get lost in the brush. Or they climb too high on a rock ledge and can't get down. Sheep need shepherds to protect them, help them find food and water, and trim their wool every year.

People are a lot like sheep. Sometimes we do silly things and get into tight spots. We need plenty of care. And we're often bad at protecting ourselves. But guess what? Jesus is our Shepherd! When we need something, we can ask Him for it. When we feel lost or confused, we can call out to Him.

Do you need your Shepherd tonight? Say, "Help me, Jesus!"

Thank You, Jesus, for watching over me.
I'm glad I have You to care for me.

SHINE YOUR LIGHT INTO THE NIGHT!

Do you know a boy or girl who is alone
or scared or stuck in a bad situation?
How can you let that person know about
the Good Shepherd who loves them?

76

SURRENDER!

And we destroy every proud thing that raises itself against the knowledge of God. We capture every thought and make it give up and obey Christ.

—2 CORINTHIANS 10:5

Imagine that you are a knight fighting the army of an evil king. The battle is fierce. Swords flash back and forth. But slowly, your army captures the enemy soldiers. Now they have to serve the good king and do what's right.

Did you know that this kind of battle happens all the time—right inside your head? Each day, your good thoughts and bad thoughts fight for your attention. You don't have swords or spears up there, but you do have a special weapon that's perfect for the job. God says His Word is like a sword with sharp edges on both sides (Hebrews 4:12). God's truth cuts down the lies that lead us to do wrong things.

To win the battle in your mind, you need to know what God says is right. Then you can say no to any thought that goes against His Word. Every time you say no to a wrong thought, you're like a knight capturing an enemy. With the Bible's help, you can make your thoughts obey God.

God, help me win the battle in my mind. I want to think good thoughts that please You.

SHINE YOUR LIGHT INTO THE NIGHT!

Look up Ephesians 6:17. What does this verse say about the sword we should use to cut down bad thoughts?

77

WITH ALL YOUR MIND

"Love the Lord your God with all
your heart, soul and mind."

—MATTHEW 22:37

When a dolphin goes to sleep, half its brain stays awake. A little later, the first half of the dolphin's brain goes to sleep, and the other half takes a turn being awake. This way, the dolphin can control its blowhole to take breaths.

Another word for *brain* is *mind*. Today's verse says we should love God with our mind—and not just half of it. Think about the ways you use your brain to learn, make decisions, and solve problems. Loving God with your mind means using it to know Him better.

Read the Bible to discover what makes God happy. Learn about animals, rocks, and outer space to see how smart and creative God is. If you're curious why God made rainbows, ask your Sunday school leader or a parent. If you struggle with a sin, memorize a Bible verse to help you resist that wrong.

God loves *all* of you. Love Him back by using your whole brain to get to know all about Him.

Dear Jesus, I want to love You with all my mind. Teach me to use it in ways that please You.

SHINE YOUR LIGHT INTO THE NIGHT!

Pretend you accidentally dropped Mom's phone into the toilet. What should you do? Use your mind to make a good decision. Now, do you have a real problem that you can solve with your mind?

78

GET DRESSED

As God's chosen people, holy and dearly loved,
clothe yourselves with compassion, kindness,
humility, gentleness and patience.

—COLOSSIANS 3:12 NIV

Chores finished? Check. Teeth brushed? Check. Face washed? Check! Now it's almost time to climb into bed. Which clothes will you choose: a swimming suit or PJs?

Even if you're excited about plans to go swimming tomorrow, PJs are a better pick for sleeping. They're soft, they're cozy, and they calm your mind for some good Zs. In the morning, you can change into whatever clothes you need for the day.

Did you know that God has given us special clothes to wear both day and night? You won't find them folded in your dresser though. These clothes are attitudes that show a love for God and others. God wants us to take off any sinful thoughts and actions and, instead, wear compassion, kindness, humility, gentleness, and patience everywhere we go.

When you get dressed in the morning or put on your PJs at night, check that you're wearing your godly clothes too. These clothes are a sign that you're following God's Spirit and that you're ready to do His work.

Father, I want to dress in the special clothes You made for me. _____ is especially hard for me. Help me wear it more often.

SHINE YOUR LIGHT INTO THE NIGHT!

Do you know what all the "clothes" in the verse are? If not, ask an adult to explain them to you.

A GOOD GUEST

Children are known by the way they act, whether their conduct is pure, and whether it is right.

—PROVERBS 20:11 NLT

Did you know that Jesus had sleepovers?

Jesus liked to visit His friends, and He often spent the night with them. In a little town called Bethany lived three of Jesus' best friends: a brother and two sisters named Lazarus, Mary, and Martha.

Sometimes Jesus stayed with them for several days. He ate, laughed, and talked with them. Sometimes He rested, and sometimes He told stories. He was a wonderful guest.

When you visit friends or family members, do you treat their furniture and other belongings carefully? If so, then you are a good guest. It's also important to thank them for meals or snacks they share with you. And make sure you don't get too rowdy.

Does Jesus really care whether you're a good guest? Of course! He's very pleased when your actions show that you're His child—even at Grandma's house!

Thank You, Jesus, for giving me friends and family who love to spend time with me. Help me be a good guest when I visit them.

SHINE YOUR LIGHT INTO THE NIGHT!

Imagine that your favorite doll or stuffed animal is spending the night with you. Pretend to share a bedtime snack or tell your toy a story. Then tuck it in, pulling the blankets snug.

80

ASK A GRANDPARENT

Ask your elders. They will inform you.

—DEUTERONOMY 32:7

Did you know that baby elephants learn lots of skills from their grandmas? Elephants live longer than most other animals. So most herds have a grandma elephant. Grandma elephants help guard the babies. They teach them how to stay safe. And they lead the herd to water and food.

You, too, can learn a lot from your grandparents and other elderly people. They are often great at board games and puzzles. They have lots of wisdom to share about problems, such as how to get along with someone who is unkind. They like to share stories that are funny, exciting, or full of history. A grandma or grandpa who loves Jesus has much to tell you about how to be a wise and happy Christian.

Elderly people have already learned many lessons. If you have a question or need help, ask a grandparent!

Jesus, thank You for grandmas and grandpas and all the things they can teach me.

SHINE YOUR LIGHT INTO THE NIGHT!

Think of a question to ask an elderly person in the next couple days, such as "What was your favorite game to play when you were little?" or "What did you like most about school when you were my age?"

81

THANK YOU!

Every good and perfect gift is from above, coming
down from the Father of the heavenly lights,
who does not change like shifting shadows.

—JAMES 1:17 NIV

When was the last time you felt really proud of yourself?
Maybe you hit a home run in a baseball game,

made a clay pot in art class, or learned a new song on the guitar. It feels great to succeed!

But the Bible says that we need to watch out. It's easy to feel big when we succeed, but we need to remember that our gifts and talents come from God. For example, if you're good at singing, who gave you your voice? If you're a good student, who gave you your brain? The truly amazing person is the God who made you.

The Bible says that every good gift we have comes from our Father, who loves us. When something good happens in our lives, we should celebrate! And in the excitement, we need to remember to give God the credit for giving us our gifts.

Dear God, I know that You are the reason I'm good at _____. Thank You!

SHINE YOUR LIGHT INTO THE NIGHT!

What is one thing you're really good at? What do you enjoy about it? Now think of one way you can use this gift to help someone else.

82

WORSHIP TIME

If you eat, or if you drink, or if you do anything,
do everything for the glory of God.

—1 CORINTHIANS 10:31

Are you ready? It's time for a worship service.

Wait, you're probably thinking. *It's time for bed, not church!*

But God invites us to a different kind of worship

service—one that lasts for our whole lives! And don't worry, you don't have to sit still. Instead, God wants you to be super active in His service.

In the Bible, God explains that real worship is the way we live. When we play, we can worship God. When we eat or drink, we can bring God glory. In our schoolwork or chores, in our sports, in our conversations and our thoughts, we can worship God. You can even worship Him by going to sleep! That's because sleeping is taking care of your body and obeying your parents. Whatever you do, do it in a way that shows God honor and shows others God's love and truth.

So what's your plan for tomorrow? No matter what the day holds, ask God to help you worship Him in every part of it.

Jesus, I want to worship You with everything I do. Help me understand how I can show Your glory through the things I do and my actions toward others.

SHINE YOUR LIGHT INTO THE NIGHT!

How can you worship God while playing with your friends tomorrow?

83

WHAT? WHEN? HOW? WHY?

But at that time, in the future, we shall see clearly. Now I know only a part. But at that time I will know fully, as God has known me.

—1 CORINTHIANS 13:12

How far away is the farthest star?
Do angels go to sleep at night?
Why can't I remember my dreams?

Do you have lots of questions? You're not alone! People have been asking questions since God made the first man and woman. Can't you picture Adam seeing an orangutan for the first time? He probably asked, "What's *that*?"

Do you have questions about God? Do you wish you understood Him better? That's great! You should learn as much as you can about Him. But there are some questions not even the smartest person in the world can answer. That's because God is so ginormous and awesome. No person can completely understand Him.

One day we'll understand much, much more. In heaven, we'll see and hug Jesus, and He'll answer our questions. But for now, it's good to wonder. God wants you to be curious. He loves it when we want to know Him better!

Dear Lord, one thing I would like to know about You is _____.

SHINE YOUR LIGHT INTO THE NIGHT!

Ask the person who's tucking you in to tell you one question he or she has about God.

84

CLIMB UP!

Those who know the Lord trust him. He will
not leave those who come to him.

—PSALM 9:10

You're spending the night at your friend's house. Your friend has a bunk bed, and you'll be sleeping on the top bunk. A wide ladder stretches up from the floor to the bed. The ladder looks safe, and your friend says that other people have climbed it. But in order to prove you trust it, you have to do more than think about it or talk about it. You have to climb up!

Our relationship with God works the same way. We can learn all about Him from the Bible and devotionals. We can listen to our preacher and our parents. We can know facts about Jesus. But if we really want a friendship with God, we have to climb the ladder of faith. We need to move from knowing about Him to trusting Him. True love trusts, and we show that we trust God by doing what He says.

Jesus, I don't want to just know about You. I want to put all my trust in You. Help me show that I trust You by obeying You each day.

SHINE YOUR LIGHT INTO THE NIGHT!

How did you show your trust of God today? How can you show it tomorrow?

85

READY FOR TAKEOFF

The person who serves God will be ready and will have everything he needs to do every good work.

—2 TIMOTHY 3:17

Do you know why bats hang by their toes to sleep? They want to be ready!

It's hard for bats to take off from a standing position. So they hang upside down. That way they are ready to drop into the air and swoop into the night. They're always ready to go.

Being ready is good. As followers of Jesus, we should be ready to do good whenever we have the chance. We should be ready to tell others about Him. We should be ready to serve people who need help. We should even be ready to obey our parents.

The best way to be ready is to practice. Practice doing the right things. The more you help others or say your prayers today, the more ready you'll be to do these things again the next day. Even if you *don't* hang from your toes!

Lord, help me be ready to do good.
When someone needs help, I want
to be the first to volunteer.

SHINE YOUR LIGHT INTO THE NIGHT!

Get ready to answer someone who
asks "Who is Jesus?" by practicing what
you'll say. Your answer doesn't have to
be fancy. "He's my best friend" or "He
forgave my sins" is a very good start!

PRAYER PATTERNS

"When you pray, you should go into your room and close the
door. Then pray to your Father who cannot be seen. Your
Father can see what is done in secret, and he will reward you."

—MATTHEW 6:6

Do you have a bedtime routine or pattern? Do you do
things in the same order each night? Maybe you first put

away your toys, then you get in the bath. Or perhaps you brush your teeth, then choose your clothes for tomorrow.

In the Bible, Daniel had a pattern of praying. Every day, at three specific times, he opened his window, knelt, and prayed. No matter what happened, Daniel stuck to his prayer pattern. And Daniel's life was full of trouble. As a young man, an army attacked his city. The soldiers forced him to move to a different land. Several times, people wanted to kill him. But Daniel trusted God to take care of him. So each day, Daniel stopped to pray.

Even when the king made a new law that people could pray only to him and not to God, Daniel stuck to his pattern and prayed. When the king threw Daniel into the lions' den for disobeying, God rescued Daniel. Daniel's prayer time made him strong so he could be brave through it all.

Jesus, I want to have a prayer pattern that makes me strong like Daniel. Remind me each day to stop and talk to You. Today I need help with _____.

SHINE YOUR LIGHT INTO THE NIGHT!

Is there something that's been hard for you lately? Tell God about it.

87

NEW WINGS

If anyone belongs to Christ, then he is made new.
The old things have gone; everything is made new!

—2 CORINTHIANS 5:17

What creature changes its body completely while it sleeps? A butterfly, of course!

A butterfly starts out as a caterpillar, then it wraps

itself up in a soft, cozy cocoon. A few weeks later, it comes out looking totally different. It has colorful wings and a long, thin body.

Butterflies give us a beautiful picture of what happens to our hearts when we trust Jesus to save us. Just like the caterpillar can't fly without wings, we can't live for God without His love in our hearts. But when we're sorry for our sins and give our lives to Jesus, a miracle happens. God makes us a whole new creation! We are no longer stuck in our sins. Like a butterfly with new wings, we soar with God's power to love and serve Him.

We can't become brand-new on our own. But we can ask God to do it. He'll wrap us up in His love and make us beautiful.

God, thank You for making me new. Help me live like the new person I am in You and not do the bad things I used to do.

SHINE YOUR LIGHT INTO THE NIGHT!

In what way would you like Jesus to make you brand-new?

88

SLEEPY JESUS

You are God's children whom he
loves. So try to be like God.

—EPHESIANS 5:1

After a long, dusty day, Jesus curled up and dozed off. With His power, Jesus healed the blind, fed thousands of people from one lunch, and silenced angry threats. But it still wore Him out!

While Jesus was on earth, He showed us how we should act. One reason He slept was that He had a human body that grew tired. But He also slept to show us that sleep is good for us.

When we read the Bible, we should pay attention to the things Jesus did and try to do them ourselves. For example, instead of bragging about Himself, Jesus talked about His Father, God. We can do that too. Instead of fussing about what He wanted and needed, He asked others what they wanted and needed. We can do that as well!

Do you want to be like Jesus? Say what He said, and do what He did. Be kind. Obey your parents. Be gentle with those who are sick. And go to sleep!

Jesus, You are the perfect example for me to follow. One way I want to be just like You is _____.

SHINE YOUR LIGHT INTO THE NIGHT!

Jesus spent time with His best friends. If you play with someone tomorrow, be sure to treat your friend like Jesus would.

89

NEVER GIVE UP

Then God will strengthen you with his own great power. And you will not give up when troubles come, but you will be patient.

—COLOSSIANS 1:11

In just a few nights, one mole can dig a tunnel as long as a football field. Moles are furry animals about the size of a potato that live underground. Their front paws are shaped like tiny shovels, just right for digging. While you sleep, moles dig . . . and dig . . . and dig. They never give up until their tunnel is finished.

Have you been trying to do something lately that's harder than you thought it would be? Maybe you're learning to tie your shoes, ride a bicycle, print neatly, or memorize a Bible verse.

God knows that some tasks aren't easy. That's why He promised to strengthen us with His great power. So when you want to give up, pray, "Lord, I can't do this by myself. I need Your power!" Always remember that it's not about being perfect; it's about trying your best.

Don't give up. Keep digging like the mighty mole!

Jesus, sometimes it's hard for me to
_____. Please make me strong
with Your power and help me succeed.

SHINE YOUR LIGHT INTO THE NIGHT!

Ask an adult to tell you about a time he or she felt like giving up. What helped that person do the difficult thing? How well can he or she do that activity now?

90

GOD'S BIG FAMILY, PART 1

From the rising of the sun to the place where it sets, the name of the LORD is to be praised.

—PSALM 113:3 NIV

Where does the sun set? Everywhere! People across the whole world see the sun rise and set each day. And all around the world, in countries near and far away, people praise God like you do. Even though their songs and ways of praying sound and look different from what you're used to, they are just as beautiful to Him.

In Mexico, people say, "Te quiero, Señor" instead of "I love You, Lord." Instead of "Praise Jesus," the people of Italy say, "Lode a Gesù." And the Germans say, "Ja, Herr" instead of "Yes, Lord!"

Everyone who loves and serves Jesus is part of the great big family of God. Somewhere on earth, there's always someone praising Him, putting a smile on His face, and stirring the love in His heart. When's the next time He'll hear you praising Him?

Jesus, thank You for letting me be part of Your big family. Bless all my brothers and sisters everywhere.

SHINE YOUR LIGHT INTO THE NIGHT!

Supplies: world map

Find Italy on the map. Then say, "Lode a Gesù." God loves hearing praises in any language!

91

GOD'S BIG FAMILY, PART 2

There were so many people that no one could count them. They were from every nation, tribe, people, and language of the earth.

—REVELATION 7:9

Do you have a quilt? A quilt is a blanket made of different pieces of fabric. By themselves, the pieces are very small. But when they're sewn together, they make a beautiful, warm cover.

God's people are like a quilt. We're all different, and each of us is special. But together, we're even better and stronger.

Imagine all the people at your church, a busy mall, or a ball game. Then multiply by a zillion. That's how many people live on earth. They come in many colors and speak many languages. There are tiny babies and great-grandmas.

You probably know only about fifty people, so it seems impossible that God knows and loves everyone on earth. But He does! Together, we are His lovely, colorful "people quilt."

God, teach me to love and care for all kinds of people, no matter how different they are from me. You love every one of us, and I want to do the same.

SHINE YOUR LIGHT INTO THE NIGHT!

Supplies: paper, crayons

You're a special part of God's big quilt. Decorate the paper so it looks like you in some way. For example, if you love purple, make it purple. If you like stripes, draw stripes.

92

DON'T FLOAT AWAY!

Cling to what is good.

—ROMANS 12:9 NIV

Is there anything that looks sillier than a walrus?

These chubby, whiskered animals have tusks that are like big, long teeth. Walruses use those tusks to do something clever when they sleep. Since they love to spend time in the cold water, they hook their tusks into the ice at bedtime. This way, they make sure they don't float away or hurt themselves while they're sleeping.

Do you ever float away from where you're supposed to be or what you're supposed to be doing? Maybe you joined kids in the neighborhood who were playing with something they're not supposed to touch. Or maybe a friend made you so mad that later you were mean to your brother.

Just like a walrus uses its tusks to keep from drifting away, you can hold tightly to God's love and teachings. They will keep you from drifting away from what is right. Cling to good as tightly as a whiskered walrus!

Dear God, give me strength to cling to what's right even when others try to pull me away.

SHINE YOUR LIGHT INTO THE NIGHT!

Do you have a friend or classmate who tries to get you to do bad things? How can you stick with doing the right thing? How can you help your friend do the right thing too?

93

CONTAGIOUS

Follow my example, as I follow the example of Christ.

—1 CORINTHIANS 11:1 NIV

Hippos yawn. Tigers yawn. Even fish yawn!

Yawns are contagious. That means they spread from one person to the next. You can catch someone's cold, and you can also catch someone's yawn. After watching someone yawn, you'll probably start yawning too. Maybe you're yawning just from reading this!

Just like a yawn can make its way around a sleepy room, other actions can spread too. When you do things that please Jesus, your friends will catch your good attitude and copy you.

Other people see you when you're sharing and when you include those who feel left out. Others watch when you obey instructions and when you talk nicely to your siblings. Sometimes this happens even when you think no one is paying attention. You have the power to spread kindness, helpfulness, joy, and faith.

In the Bible, Paul told his students that they should follow his example because he was following Jesus. Be sure to follow Jesus, and then be a good example to others. Be contagious!

Jesus, help me be a contagious Christian. But first, help me follow Your perfect example.

SHINE YOUR LIGHT INTO THE NIGHT!

In front of a parent or sibling, pretend to yawn. Then count how long it takes for them to "catch" your yawn. Tomorrow, share this trick with someone and tell them about being contagious for Jesus.

94

METEOR MIND

And God's peace will keep your hearts and
minds in Christ Jesus. The peace that God gives
is so great that we cannot understand it.

—PHILIPPIANS 4:7

Whoooosh! Zzzooom! Sometimes at night, you can
see streaks of light racing across the sky. That's a

meteor shower. Meteor showers are caused by lots of little pieces of rock and dust from a passing comet.

Have you ever felt as if you have a meteor shower in your brain? You try to sleep, but worries shoot across your mind! It can be hard to calm down, but Jesus can help. One day, He told His friends, "My peace I give you. . . . So don't let your hearts be troubled" (John 14:27). You're His friend too. And He wants to share His peace with you.

Look back on the day. Did anything bother or scare you? Tell God about It. He can handle anything.

Now list the blessings of the day. What are some ways Jesus showed you His love? What happened to make you smile or laugh? Thank Him for each blessing.

When you talk to Jesus, He will give you His peace. Now lie back on your pillow and relax. Good night!

Jesus, thank You for listening to me. Help me remember to talk to You when I am worried.

SHINE YOUR LIGHT INTO THE NIGHT!

Think of one way you can help Mom or Dad have a more peaceful morning.

95

OOPS!

I do not mean that I am already as God wants me to be. I have not yet reached that goal. But I continue trying to reach it and to make it mine.

—PHILIPPIANS 3:12

Light bulbs have one job: to light things up when it's dark. But the man who invented them, Thomas Edison, made 2,298 mistakes before figuring out how to make light bulbs work.

Mr. Edison said that out of his three thousand ideas of how to make a light bulb, only two were right. Yet because of him, we have lamps and night-lights and flashlights. Aren't you glad he kept trying?

Sometimes we make mistakes. Sometimes these happen when we aren't paying attention. Or we think we know how to do something, but we really don't. Or we do or say the wrong thing without meaning to. *Everyone* makes mistakes—even grown-ups! They've had many years to learn, yet they still goof from time to time.

The next time you goof, remember that Jesus loves you no matter what. When you try to spell a word using the wrong letters or put your shoes on the wrong feet, Jesus doesn't think you're silly. Instead, He's proud of you for trying!

Dear Jesus, I'm not very good at
_____. Thank You for being proud
of me for trying, and help me keep learning.

SHINE YOUR LIGHT INTO THE NIGHT!

Ask an adult to tell you about a time he or she made a mistake but learned something new from the experience.

96

SEEK AND FIND

"You will search for me. And when you search
for me with all your heart, you will find me!"

—JEREMIAH 29:13

Shhh! Do you hear that? There's a bunny hopping in
the grass, a mole digging in the garden, and a mouse
munching on a snack. You probably can't hear these
sounds, but a fox can.

Foxes hunt during the quiet night because they use their excellent hearing to find prey. A fox can hear a mouse digging underground from two blocks away! When the fox hears its prey, it follows the sound to the right place. Then the fox digs until it finds what it's searching for: dinner!

Jesus said that if we search for Him, we'll discover Him. But we don't need super hearing or X-ray vision. Jesus is easy to find.

You can find Jesus in the Bible because it contains His own words. You can find Him when you do something kind because you're doing His work. You can find Him through prayer too. Anything we do that helps us love or know Jesus better is a way of finding Him. Where have you looked for Jesus lately?

Dear Jesus, thank You for being easy to find. You are the best Friend ever!

SHINE YOUR LIGHT INTO THE NIGHT!

Tonight, search for Jesus in a song. Quietly sing your favorite worship tune. Do you feel peace or happiness in your heart? That's Jesus. You've found Him!

97

DOS AND DON'TS

The Lord's orders are right. They make people happy.
The Lord's commands are pure. They light up the way.

—PSALM 19:8

It's time for the bedtime dos and don'ts.

Do fluff your pillow.

Don't stand on your head.

Don't put on your rain boots.

Do you wish all rules were this easy to follow? You may not always like rules, but they keep you safe. For example, your parents might ask you to turn off your tablet at bedtime. This rule helps you sleep, something your body and mind need. Your parents make the rule to take care of you.

Sometimes we don't like God's rules either. But they, too, are made out of love. God tells us to forgive quickly because He knows our hearts are happy when we're at peace with others. He wants us to tell the truth because lying hurts us and others.

God wants to protect you. He has made rules to keep you safe because He loves you so much!

Dear God, help me remember that rules keep me safe. Thank You for adults who care about me.

SHINE YOUR LIGHT INTO THE NIGHT!

Is there a family rule that you've been slow to obey? Ask your parents to help you understand the reason for it. Then thank them for taking care of you.

98

TINY PRAYERS

Never stop praying.

—1 THESSALONIANS 5:17

Ants go to sleep 250 times every day! Scientists used to think that fire ants never slept. But now they know these ants actually take hundreds of tiny naps every day. There's something we, too, can do for a minute here and a minute there, all day long: talk to Jesus. When you pray, it's nice to sit down, close your eyes, and fold your hands. But you don't have to.

You can have tiny prayers with Jesus at any moment. You can talk to Him when you're playing with friends, helping Mom at the grocery store, or fishing with Grandpa. Do you need help with an addition problem? Say, "Please help me focus, Jesus." Are you feeling grumpy? Tell Him about it. Are you excited because it's snowing? Say, "Thank You, Jesus, for snowflakes!"

Is there someone who makes you happy every time you hear from him or her? Jesus feels that way about you. Even if you talked with Him 250 times in one day, He'd never get tired of hearing from you!

Jesus, thank You that You're
always happy to hear from me.

SHINE YOUR LIGHT INTO THE NIGHT!

Did something make you laugh today? Did you play a fun game? Did something frustrate you? Tomorrow, remember that Jesus wants to hear about everything. And you don't have to wait for bedtime to tell Him about it.

99

NEVER ANOTHER

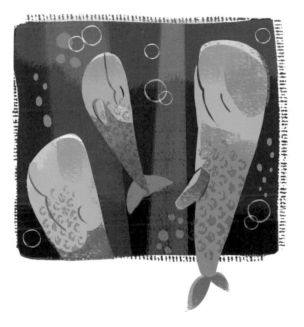

We know the love that God has for us,
and we trust that love. God is love.

—1 JOHN 4:16

When scientists first discovered how sperm whales
sleep, they were amazed! Most whales take little

naps while floating on their bellies. But sperm whales sleep with their noses pointing toward the surface of the water, like enormous bowling pins bobbing around in the sea.

Maybe there are things you do differently too. Maybe your whole family is right-handed, but you're left-handed. Maybe all your friends like playing tag, but you would much rather read a book. It's okay to be different!

Many of God's people in the Bible were unusual. John the Baptist lived in the wilderness, ate bugs and honey, and wore clothes made of camel's hair. But Jesus was very pleased with him.

If people were all the same, the world would be a boring place. But God created each one of us to be special in our own way. He never makes two people the same—not even twins. There will never be another you!

Lord, I know that one way I'm different from a lot of people is _____.
Thank You for making me special!

SHINE YOUR LIGHT INTO THE NIGHT!

Think of three people who make you happy. What makes each one different? Tomorrow, tell them why you think they're great.

100

HAPPILY EVER AFTER

I heard a loud voice from the throne. The voice said, "Now God's home is with men. He will live with them, and they will be his people. God himself will be with them and will be their God. He will wipe away every tear from their eyes. There will be no more death, sadness, crying, or pain. All the old ways are gone."

—REVELATION 21:3–4

Congratulations! You've reached the end of this book. What was your favorite devotion?

The Bible has an ending too. The last book of the Bible is called Revelation. The apostle John wrote Revelation to tell how God's story about us ends.

John described a vision of the future that God showed him. Parts of it are hard to understand, but the main idea is clear: Jesus is coming back one day to take His people home to heaven! All sadness, sin, and death will end. Christians will live in perfect joy and peace with Jesus.

We know that God always keeps His promises, so we need to be ready for Jesus to return. Have you given your life to Jesus? If not, just pray. Ask God to forgive your sins. Tell Him you trust in Jesus and want Him to be your Savior. When we give our lives to Jesus, the real adventure begins. You will spend the best happily ever after with Him forever.

Jesus, I've done things my way, and I'm sorry. I know You died on the cross to save me and forgive me. Now I want to obey You with all my heart. Thank You!

SHINE YOUR LIGHT INTO THE NIGHT!

What are you looking forward to in heaven? Think of someone who needs to hear about all the exciting things there. Tell them tomorrow.